SEEING CLEARLY

A MEMOIR OF VISION LOSS, EMOTIONAL
BLINDNESS, AND FINDING MY TRUE SELF

CHRISTOPHER T. MONNETTE

Copyright © 2022 Christopher T. Monnette
All rights reserved.

All rights reserved. No portion of this book may be reproduced in any form without permission from the publisher, except as permitted by U.S. copyright law.

DISCLAIMER

This is a work of creative nonfiction. The author has made every attempt to accurately portray the events in this book to the best of his memory. The conversations in this book come from the author's recollection and are not intended to be a word-for-word transcript of the actual dialog. Rather, the author has retold them in a way that represents the emotions and meanings of what was said. Some of the names have been changed, and some events have been compressed.

Paperback ISBN: 978-0-578-38513-6

https://chrismonnette.com

Dedication

To my daughter, Jennifer, and, my son, Jonathan who were the source of my inspiration for this journey of self-discovery. To my wife, Marilyn, who welcomed me into her heart and her life when I wasn't sure I deserved it, and to my brother, Mike, who has always been a model for the man I wanted to be.

Contents

1 A Blurring World　　　　　1

2 The Diagnosis　　　　　　9

3 An Unexpected Gift　　　　26

4 A New Language　　　　　41

5 Lucky Thirteen　　　　　　54

6 Italian Driving　　　　　　67

7 Mutual Assured Destruction　82

8 A Glimpse Of Happiness　　95

9 The Beginning of an End　　113

10 Always　　　　　　　　　125

11 A Great Teacher　　　　　140

12 Rock Bottom　　　　　　　153

13 Long and Winding Road　　168

1

A Blurring World

I HAVE HEARD THAT GETTING MARRIED on a rainy day is bad luck. I am not so sure. I was married twice on bright, sunny days, and both ended in divorce, but this time, it was different. It was pouring rain on July 13, 2013, as Marilyn and I recited our vows, hastily huddled inside, in the corner of the Chautauqua Dining Hall in Boulder, Colorado. The years leading up to that day were the darkest period of my life, and as the skies cleared that night it was as if the storm had washed away the pain of that difficult time. As we began our life together, our future was clear and bright, but before our honeymoon ended, there was already another cloud beginning to obscure the road before us.

It was early afternoon on July 17 when Marilyn and I picked up our rental car at the airport in Catania, on the northeast coast of Sicily, where we began our honeymoon. We had plans to spend the first two nights at the Grand Timeo Hotel, about an hour to the north in Taormina, and then work our way to Palermo on the northwest coast for our flight home.

Dating back to before 345 BC, Taormina is an ancient village built into the side of steep hills rising 820 feet from the Mediterranean Sea. Laced throughout the hillside is a maze of narrow, meandering cobblestone streets densely packed with ancient homes and shops that have somehow managed to defy gravity for centuries. The Grand Timeo is located at one of the highest points in Taormina with sprawling views of the city and sea below. The hotel, like most of the structures in Taormina, was built into the side of the hill. Directly above it sat the Teatro Antico di Taormina, an Ancient Greek amphitheater, that had been the inspiration for the Red Rocks Amphitheater back home in Colorado.

We rented a Volkswagen Jetta at the airport in Catania and started the hour-long drive to Taormina. I drove. Marilyn was navigating using Google Maps on my iPhone. There were two things wrong with that: I was driving, and she was navigating. I am far more comfortable with technology and navigation than my wife. She is far more comfortable in control.

We drove for about forty-five minutes before getting off the highway, only five miles as the crow flies from our destination. We would be taking a longer route. You could tell from the steep terrain around us that the road was clearly going to be a winding one. As we got off the highway, many of the "roads" that Google insisted we turn on looked more like sidewalks or driveways.

"Make the next right," Marilyn told me.

"Okay," I said, and then drove right past the tiny strip of pavement or cobblestone looking for an actual road.

"You missed it!"

"No way. Are you sure you are reading the map right?" I protested.

"Yes! Yes! Make the next left."

"Where?"

"You missed it again!"

I am not sure who cried uncle first, but we had both had enough.

Seeing Clearly

"Let me drive!" she said.

"Let me navigate."

"Yes, please!"

I moved to the right seat and picked up my iPhone and immediately noticed two things. First, even with my glasses on, the map was blurry. It was still readable but, clearly, I needed to get a new prescription when I got home. Perhaps it was just the jet lag. We were both exhausted. A good night's sleep was probably what I needed. Besides, we had a bigger issue: the battery on my iPhone was at less than ten percent and we had no printed map. Google Maps was all we had, and I had failed to bring a car charger for my iPhone. We needed to find that hotel, quickly!

With my wife and I now in our proper places the situation improved. Tension in the car dropped a few levels from DEFCON 1, where we had been just minutes before. Warfare was no longer imminent. We just needed to get to the hotel.

With tired eyes, reading the map on the small iPhone screen was a hassle, and to make matters worse there was nothing intuitive about the layout of the roads in a city built on the side of a mountain more than two thousand years ago.

Now it was my turn. As Marilyn drove, I would announce, "The road is coming up on the right."

"Where? I don't see it!"

"Right here! Right *here*! You missed it! Okay, keep going—we'll get the next one."

I looked at the screen on my iPhone: *Recalculating Route... Battery 8%.*

"Okay, right around this corner turn left."

"HERE? That's not a street!"

The battery on my iPhone dropped to 6%.

"It has to be!"

At one point, after making it into the heart of the ancient city where our hotel was located, the road squeezed through an archway between two structures. The opening was so narrow that we could barely fit a finger between the sideview mirrors and the walls on either side. Marilyn drove about halfway through the opening and then stopped.

"Baby, what are you doing? You can't stop here."

She wouldn't go forward. She wouldn't go back. "I can't. I can't!"

There was no way to open the door to get out and help her. She was frozen.

Five percent.

A car pulled up behind us and honked impatiently.

DEFCON 1.

With all the commotion, an older gentleman—a local resident, I assumed—suddenly appeared. Seeing the situation, he gave my wife an encouraging smile and, using hand gestures, carefully coaxed her out of the archway.

After that, it only took a couple of laps around the city center until we got to what appeared to be a pedestrian walkway packed with people, at the end of which, a hundred yards away, sat our hotel. That was it for Marilyn. She refused to drive through the road of people. She'd had enough. We both had. I got out and walked. The doorman followed me back and drove the car the last hundred yards.

The drive from the airport had been miles. The first thirty-five were uneventful. The last five were among the most harrowing driving experiences either of us had ever had.

The hotel and the city of Taormina were worth every bit of it.

From the balcony off our room, we had the most amazing views overlooking the historic city below and the Mediterranean Sea. For dinner we sat outside on the veranda off the dining room. The food was amazing. The wine was fantastic. Exactly what we had hoped for when we planned our honeymoon. After dinner that evening,

Seeing Clearly

we returned to our room to find rose pedals on the floor leading to the bed and floating in the bathtub.

The next morning, I woke up rested and relaxed. Ready for our vacation to begin in earnest. My eyes were still tired. Nothing to worry about, though. It had been a tough travel day. I was sure that with some coffee and less stress, things would be fine. We didn't discuss it. There was nothing to talk about. I just needed a little rest.

Over the next ten days, as we made our way across Sicily, my vision seemed to get a little worse each day. By the time we got to Palermo ten days later we both knew that something was wrong. My vision had changed substantially since we'd left the United States. Marilyn and I talked about what was happening, but I downplayed how bad my eyesight had become. Why worry her?

What was most frightening to me was the fact that whatever was going on was impacting both eyes. Few things scare me more than not knowing the facts. My degree is in electrical engineering, so I began to troubleshoot the problem quietly in my mind.

Think it through, Chris. Start at the beginning and trace the circuit back...

The eyes are independent of each other. Each eye has a cornea that focuses light on the retina at the back of the eye where there are millions of photo-sensitive cells known as rods and cones. Those photo-sensitive cells convert the light to electrical signals that are in turn transmitted by an optic nerve to the brain.

The fact that I was having a problem with both eyes seemed to rule out an issue with my corneas. To the best of my knowledge, I had not been injured in any way. I felt no pain or discomfort in my eyes, nor were there any visual signs of infection such as redness or watering. Maybe something could suddenly go wrong with one eye, but both at the same time? It just seemed that it must be something else. And why so suddenly? It made no sense to me, but what the hell did I know? I was an engineer, not a doctor.

If it wasn't my corneas, my retinas, or my optic nerves, what else could it be? I could think of only one thing that connected both eyes: the brain.

A brain tumor! What else could it possibly be? That would explain everything...

In the instant it took for that thought to form, my vision was no longer my primary concern.

As we spent the last day of our honeymoon in Palermo it was becoming nearly impossible to keep the anxiety I was feeling about my eyesight to myself. Marilyn knew that things were worse than I was willing to admit, and she insisted that we at least talk to a doctor, so we called her optometrist back in Boulder. I explained my symptoms. He asked several questions.

"Do you see flashes of light?"

"No."

"Is it both eyes or just one?"

"Both."

"Are you having headaches?"

"No."

I shared my brain tumor theory, hoping he would rule that out completely.

"It's a possibility, but I would expect headaches if that were the case." It was the best he could give me.

"I don't think it's a medical emergency," he said. "I think you can wait until you get back to the States, but see someone as soon as you do."

We thanked him and then looked at each other. There was no hiding it from Marilyn anymore. Something was wrong and I could see she was frightened. I tried to reassure her. I needed to be strong for her. Or was I just afraid to give way to the growing terror inside me?

It was well before sunrise the next morning when Marilyn and I

Seeing Clearly

pulled up to the airport in Palermo for our flight home. The rental car return was not far from the terminal, but it was too far to walk with all our luggage and there was no shuttle. Someone had to wait with the bags while the other returned the car.

I insisted that I return the car and she wait with the bags. The return lot and the walk back were both dark and I didn't like the idea of her doing that alone. The return lot was an easy drive from the terminal. We'd even practiced it together when we first arrived at the airport, just to be sure. As we did, I carefully memorized the turns so I could maintain the charade that things were not so bad for just a little longer. Look for the large yellow sign on the right, then drive a hundred feet and turn left. Drive straight for a couple hundred yards. Watch for the fenced-in parking area on the left. Turn left before you get there. Then, finally, a right into the parking lot. Missing either of the first two left turns would be a disaster, as they both appeared to lead away from the airport. The world around me was blurry, my night vision horrible. I had no idea where those roads led, all the signs were in Italian, and there was no way I could drive and use my iPhone to navigate by myself. At least the third turn was easy; if I missed that it would take me back to where I'd dropped off Marilyn, and I could start over.

Two lefts and a right into the parking lot. Then walk along the sidewalk back to the terminal. Piece of cake.

As I approached the first turn, I was driving half the speed of the cars around me. I was not going to miss that turn! And I made it successfully. One more to go. But what if I missed it? What would I do then? I tried to think through the plan just in case. Better to know what you must do than to make it up on the run. The first thing I would do is pull off to the side of the road and stop to get my bearings. Maybe see if I could back up. Worst case, I would leave the car on the side of the road and walk back for help. Then I would...

Focus, Chris! Don't miss this turn.

I continued creeping along at a snail's pace as I successfully navigated the second and final left. The parking lot was on my right. I could see all the rental cars there. I just needed to find the entry and I was home free.

I was never so happy to see my wife as when I got back to the terminal. I could tell by the look on her face that she felt the same way.

Driving off into the dark by myself that morning was an act of ignorance. Not of the physical risks—getting lost or hitting someone. Those were obvious. What I was completely ignorant of were the forces that were driving me to take the risk in the first place. I was literally and figuratively acting blindly.

I had learned at a very early age to see vulnerability as a weakness. To me, the fear of appearing vulnerable in front of my new wife was somehow more frightening than the risk of driving off into the dark with compromised vision.

I could not have imagined at the time how the challenge I was beginning to experience with my eyesight would be my biggest lesson in the power of vulnerability and would take me on a journey of discovery that would forever change the way I would see the world around me.

2

The Diagnosis

Our flight home from Sicily landed in Denver at 4 p.m. on Friday, July 26. I scheduled an appointment with the one optometrist in Boulder whom I could get in to see first thing on Saturday morning. Marilyn's optometrist, whom we had called from Sicily, wasn't available, and I didn't have a regular eye doctor because I had only been in Boulder a short time.

The optometrist we saw that morning was warm and personable. Her compassion was evident as I told her the story of the last couple weeks. It didn't take a long examination for her to realize that what was happening with me would require the care of a specialist. What she didn't tell me was that I would need to see this specialist for much more than a single visit. It would be the start of a long-term relationship.

"There are a couple of great retina specialists here in Boulder, but there is one who I think would be perfect for you. Her name is Geeta Lalwani. She is originally from Boulder and just returned here to open a practice following a surgical retina fellowship at the Bascom Palmer Eye Institute in Miami. She has awesome credentials. I think you would really like her."

"She sounds great."

"She is, and one of the things I really like about her is she is just so genuine, warm, and compassionate. I think she would be a great fit for you."

It was clear that Dr. Lalwani had touched her in some way and that, after seeing what was happening in my eyes and knowing what the treatment for my condition would likely be, she knew I would need someone with more than a little compassion. She didn't give me a clear diagnosis. She wanted Dr. Lalwani to verify what I suspect she already knew. There was some good news, though: She seemed convinced that the issue was in my eyes, not my brain.

After fourteen hours on an airplane, with little to do but think about all the possible outcomes, the thought of a brain tumor was never far from my mind. Yet, after speaking with the optometrist, I don't recall feeling any relief. I can still see the look on her face as I left her office that morning. It was a half-smile that said, "Don't worry, everything will be all right," but she also knew there would be bad news. Clearly, there was something very wrong with my eyes.

I could only imagine what Marilyn must have felt. After being single for forty-nine years she finally finds a man with whom she wants to spend the rest of her life, and two weeks after marrying him—this! The truth is, I was probably projecting my feelings more than sensing hers. I was scared. Something was seriously wrong with my eyes, and I had no idea what that would mean for me, how it would change my life. I was taught to be strong. How could I be both strong and blind?

Marilyn is the most positive person I know. When she looks at the future, all she sees are possibilities. It is one of the things I love about her most. I like to think that I see possibilities as well. I am just more keenly aware of all the things that could go wrong along the way. One of the best examples of the difference between us is how we approach parking.

When I pull into a crowded parking lot, I tend to take the first available spot even if it is toward the back. I know there might be a closer spot available, but what if there isn't and I have to drive back? By then the original spot might be taken. Even if it isn't, in the time it takes to drive to the front, look for a place, and drive back to find a new place, I could just as easily have walked. Yeah, there may be an open spot up front, but why take that chance? For me, it is a decision based on facts and data.

Marilyn, on the other hand, always drives immediately to the front row. She spends little time thinking about the prospect of not finding an available parking space. All she sees is how great it will be to have a parking spot right up front. All she can see are the possibilities. "I have parking karma," she says—and she does. In all the time I have known her, she is right far more often than not.

As we left the optometrist's office that day, Marilyn was worried, but she knew everything was going to be fine. She had faith. She had "parking karma." I was less sure. I didn't have enough information to come to that conclusion. In fact, the evidence suggested the opposite. As Neil deGrasse Tyson says, "The good thing about science is that it's true whether or not you believe in it." I was terrified and needed to understand the science behind what was happening. I needed a diagnosis. I didn't have Marilyn's parking karma.

Four days later, on July 30, I was sitting in Dr. Lalwani's office, one of her first patients in her office space. There were two people in the office: Dr. Lalwani and a receptionist. At the time, I had no idea how much the practice would grow and flourish during the years of our association.

I liked Dr. Lalwani the moment I met her. My optometrist was right; I could immediately feel her warmth, compassion, and sense of humor, all of which put me at ease. Somehow, I knew instantly that I could trust her. She may have been just starting her practice, but I could tell she knew what she was talking about.

At six-foot-four and 215 pounds, I towered over her petite frame as she led me to the examination room. After a barrage of questions, she started with a visual acuity test.

"Cover your right eye and tell me what line you can read clearly," she said as I stared at the eye chart on the wall in front of me.

"None of them," I said.

"How about this one?"

"Nope."

"Interesting. Let's try this," she said as she put up the large E.

"Yep, I can read that, but it's not very clear."

"Okay," she said. I searched her face for a reaction and saw nothing more than intellectual curiosity. If she was concerned, she hid it well.

My eyes have always been extremely sensitive. I hate putting anything in them. I could never wear contacts. Even putting in eyedrops is a chore, as I need several attempts to get in even a single drop. I remember my college roommate teasing me one day as I was trying to put some in. "I had no idea you were going to wash your face. Do you want a bar of soap with that?"

As Dr. Lalwani attempted to put eyedrops in to dilate my pupils, my eyelid snapped shut and she missed.

"Chris, look up here and relax," she said, missing again. By the third drop, she was on to me and held my lid open. "I think I got some in that time."

"Follow me, Chris," she said, and led me to another room. On the table was a futuristic-looking white box with rounded corners, about four feet tall and three feet wide. Some sort of medical instrument. On the front was what appeared to be a small camera lens and a place for my chin and forehead to rest.

Seeing Clearly

"What is this?" I asked

"An Optical Coherence Tomography, or OCT. It lets me look at a cross-section of your retina, the back of your eye where all the photoreceptors are."

I sat down and focused my left eye through the lens.

"Just keep your eye focused on the green cross in the middle," she told me.

"What green cross?" I couldn't see anything.

"Okay, no problem. Just look straight ahead and don't blink."

I saw a light move across the screen. Clearly the device was scanning my eye. It stopped and we repeated the process with the right eye. Dr. Lalwani pressed a few buttons on a keyboard as she looked at a monitor in front of her where there was a black and white image, much like an X-ray. It looked like a cross-section of a lunar landscape, undulating layers with lumps and bumps and bubbles. Nothing particularly smooth or flowing, as I would later learn is the expectation for a normal retina.

"Interesting," she said. "Follow me."

Was I sensing a bit more urgency in her voice? There were so many questions I wanted to ask her, but I didn't, not yet, because I was afraid of the answers I would get. After seeing the optometrist a few days ago, I had spent hours doing what most doctors must hate, Googling my symptoms. If she had a diagnosis for me, she wasn't saying anything yet. But I could tell something serious was going on. She was very focused and all business now. I followed quietly as she led me back to the first examination room.

I sat in front of what looked like a microscope turned sideways. Our faces were only a foot apart as she scanned the back of my eye. I looked again for concern on her face. Even at this close range all I saw was intensity. She was paying close attention.

"Interesting," she said again. "I want to do a fluorescein angiography. Do you know what that is?"

"Sounds familiar, but no," I said. "What is it?"

"It's a test that allows me to look at the blood flow in your retina. I use a special camera to take pictures of your eyes while a dye is injected into an IV in your hand. I think it can tell me a lot about what's going on."

Ugh, an IV! I hate needles. "Oh yeah. I had that test once before, several years ago when I lived in Eugene, Oregon."

"Really! Why did they do the test?"

"An ophthalmologist saw some spotting or something on the back of my eye and referred me to a retina specialist for the test."

"Very interesting. What did they find?"

"As I recall, he said they were Drusen deposits. He told me not to worry about it. Most likely some hereditary spotting."

I remember him telling me that Drusen are small, yellow fatty deposits found in the back of the eye. It is believed that they are a natural waste product from the cells that, for some reason, isn't removed in the normal course of things. By itself, the presence of Drusen isn't a big deal.

"When was this?" Dr. Lalwani asked.

"Six or seven years ago. I don't remember exactly."

"Well, I think we should do the test again if you are okay with it."

"If you think it will help. I do remember one other thing."

"What's that?"

"I don't know if they finished the test. I threw up not too long after they injected the dye."

"That can happen. Some people have reactions from the dye. Just let me know if you feel bad and we can stop."

Dr. Lalwani suggested that Marilyn have a seat in the waiting room while she conducted the test and led me into a third examination room. On the table was another device, not too different from the microscope-like device except this one had what appeared to be a camera attached to it. It immediately brought back bad memories from my first test in Eugene.

I hope I don't puke this time.

She sat me at the table in front of the device and inserted the IV into a vein in the back of my hand.

"I'll take a few test shots to get started before we inject the dye."

She had me place my chin and forehead on a metal frame on the front of the device and turned out the lights in the room. She took several shots of each eye and with each shot the camera's flash seemed more like an explosion. After eight or ten flashes I heard her voice from the dark, somewhere right in front of me. "I am going to inject the dye now, Chris." Then more bursts of light from the camera as she took another series of photographs.

As the dye began to flow through my veins the flashes were happening in rapid succession. I had no idea how many shots she'd taken when a familiar, clammy, lightheaded feeling started to wash over me. "Dr. Lalwani, I, uh…I don't feel good."

"I'm almost done. Hang in there. Just a few more shots."

I shifted my weight forward, pressing my forehead into the frame it was resting against. If I passed out, maybe I would stay locked in place and not fall out of the chair.

The flashes seemed almost constant as everything started to spin around me faster and faster with each flash until the spinning finally stopped.

Oh, thank God that's over.

Then I heard Dr. Lalwani's voice, somehow above me now. "Chris! Are you okay?"

I opened my eyes and realized that my six-four body was lying half on the floor and half on my petite doctor's lap. As she helped me sit up, she said with a nervous laugh, "Umm, I think I was supposed to have you sign a waiver saying this might happen."

I couldn't help but laugh. I was embarrassed about passing out. She was concerned about a waiver.

After my head cleared and she had an opportunity to review the images she took, she retrieved my wife from the waiting room and sat us down to share her diagnosis.

"Chris, the cause of your vision loss is macular degeneration. Do you know what that is?"

"Sort of. My brother was diagnosed with it six or seven years ago."

"Really? How old is he?"

"He's sixty-three, seven years older than me. Why?"

"It is very rare for someone your age. It is far more common for people in their seventies, but the fact that both you and your brother developed this at such a young age suggests that this may not be what is typically referred to as age-related macular degeneration, or AMD. Although that probably doesn't make a big difference. The prognosis and the treatment are the same either way."

I recall little about what I was feeling as I heard the news. I'm sure there was at least some relief that I had a name for what I was experiencing. Not knowing the facts is what I fear most. I'm far more capable dealing with adversity when I have all the information. Facts comfort me, even when the answers are scary. After my diagnosis, I needed to know more. What was a macula and what happened when it degenerated? What caused the degeneration to happen? Why was it impacting both eyes? Why was the change in my vision so sudden?

As we sat with Dr. Lalwani and talked about my diagnosis, we got a crash course on the human eye and what was happening in mine. The retina is the thin layer at the back of the eye that contains all the photo-sensitive cells that allow you to see. There are two types of cells known as rods and cones. Rods are primarily used for peripheral vision; they help us see motion and are well suited for adapting to night vision, but they cannot transmit sharp images or vivid colors. That's what the cones do. Cones are located at the center of the retina in what is called the macula. When you look at something, such as the words you're reading right now, you are using the cones located in your macula.

Macular degeneration is the leading cause of severe and permanent vision loss for people over sixty. It affects 11 million people in America alone. It's a progressive and irreversible disease that causes the cells in the macula to die. Light makes it through the cornea fine, but it is focused on dead cells. As more cells die, less light is converted to electrical signals for the brain to "see." There is no cure or treatment for macular degeneration. A special vitamin, AREDS-2, has been shown to slow the progress of the disease, but that is the best my doctor could offer me.

For me, the prognosis was clear. Someday, I would lose all my central vision and along with it the ability to read, drive a car, recognize faces, and see objects in fine detail. If there was a bright spot, it was that my peripheral vision would be unaffected, but the images provided by the rods located there are rather low resolution. Absent some new medical advancement, I would someday be legally blind.

For Marilyn, Dr. Lalwani's prognosis was only one possible outcome; she had parking karma. She believed that they would find a cure, or that I would somehow cure myself.

"Miracles happen every day, baby" is a line she has repeated many times since then.

As we sat in the office that day, we were both scared, but Marilyn saw a bright, hopeful future. I couldn't see that. With each new fact, the reality of my situation became clearer, and Dr. Lalwani still had not given me the full picture. There was more.

"Chris, you have likely had macular degeneration for years. Your right eye is pretty advanced. It is likely that the spotting the previous doctor saw in your retina several years ago was the beginning. As your right eye has gotten worse over the years, your left eye has helped compensate, filling in the gaps in your vision. Your brain uses the images from both eyes to create the complete picture you see."

"Why the sudden change then?" I asked.

"Well, in about ten percent of the cases of macular degeneration, as the cells in the macula die, the body tries to repair itself by producing a protein called VEGF, which signals the body to grow small blood vessels to bring oxygen and nutrients to the affected area. That works elsewhere in your body, like if you have a torn muscle or something like that, but it doesn't work for your retina. It causes small, leaky blood vessels to grow under your retina, which results in sudden and significant loss of vision. It's called wet, or neovascular, macular degeneration."

"And that's happening with me?"

"In your left eye for sure. I could see that in the images I took, and probably in the right eye as well—it's hard to tell. I couldn't get a good image of that eye before you passed out. It is why your eyesight changed so dramatically in such a short time. With your right eye already compromised you were dependent on your left. Once that was affected you had nothing else to fall back on."

"So, what does all that mean?"

"Wet macular degeneration may only be ten percent of the cases, but it probably accounts for ninety percent of those who become legally blind because of the disease."

With each bit of news, it was becoming more and more clear to me that there was no parking space up front this time.

"Chris, the good news is that while I can't do anything to prevent the progression of the dry, there is a very effective treatment for the wet, and with prompt treatment, you will likely regain most, if not all, of the vision you have lost over the last couple weeks."

As she walked me through the diagnosis, I was concerned but comforted by the understanding of what was happening. The knowledge that there was an effective treatment for the dramatic vision loss I had experienced over the last two weeks was a relief, but it was short-lived.

Seeing Clearly

As she explained the treatment, I could hardly breathe. It involved injecting a biological anti-VEGF drug, Avastin, directly into my eye, while I was awake and watching.

"I know it sounds scary, Chris, but it is actually not at all painful. I will numb your eye. It is a relatively routine procedure. The biggest risk is infection, and we will take plenty of precautions to protect against that.

"I can't tell you how long you have before you lose all of your central vision as a result of the dry macular degeneration, but I can tell you this: If you do not get these treatments soon, it will happen in weeks, maybe months, not years, and if you wait too long, there will be nothing I can do to help you."

"So will the injections cure me?"

"No, I am sorry. The drug typically lasts for only about a month."

"I have to come back in a month and get more injections? How long do I have to do that?"

"I wish I could tell you. You may need to get injections every month for the rest of your life. We will need to see how it goes after a few months. And Chris, this is only treating the wet macular degeneration. The underlying dry will continue to progress slowly. There are some promising drugs in development to prevent the further progression of the disease but there are no treatments for that today and nothing on the horizon to restore the vision that is lost. I wish I had better news."

Dr. Lalwani wouldn't tell me how long before I lost all my central vision. She wouldn't even venture a guess. The best she could offer was, "Every case is different, but since he was diagnosed seven years before you, your brother's progression may give you some sense of what to expect."

At the time I didn't realize the gravity of her words, how the changes my brother would experience over the years would be, in many ways, a catalyst for change in my own life.

Intellectually, I knew there was no choice—I had to get the injections. My vision over the last two weeks had changed dramatically, and the thought of being legally blind was frightening. Yet, it took me a few minutes to muster up the courage to say, "Okay."

"Good. I'll be right back." She left the room to get the drug she would be injecting into each of my eyes.

I sat in the chair looking across the room at my wife. She looked at me and simply said, "You will be okay."

All I could respond with was a nod and a half-smile.

I couldn't watch as the doctor prepared the instruments for the procedure. Seeing the needle she would use to inject my eye was more than I was prepared to deal with.

I sat there looking at my wife, fighting to control panic from overcoming me and trying to hide how frightened I was. With all my heart I wanted to run out the door, but I knew I couldn't. I reassured myself by thinking about the thousands of people who got this treatment every year. It couldn't be as horrific as I feared, but for the life of me I couldn't imagine how Dr. Lalwani would be able to stick a needle in my eye while I was awake and watching. It was terrifying.

She knew how frightened I was. Her calm and confidence reassured me just enough to keep me in the chair. She carefully and patiently explained every step, giving me as much time as I needed to ask questions.

First, she put drops in my eyes to numb them. Again, I made it hard on her, closing my eye just before the drops made it to the intended target.

How the hell am I going to keep my eye open when she sticks the needle in?

Next, she put in an orange liquid called betadine. "What does that do?" I asked.

"It helps prevent infection."

Seeing Clearly

"What happens if my eye gets infected?"

"It could be catastrophic," she said.

I didn't ask for clarification. I'd had enough bad news today.

"Okay, Chris, hold still. I am going to give you an injection of lidocaine just under your eyelid to numb your eye."

Two injections? "Isn't that what the first eyedrops were?"

"Yes, they were numbing drops, but this is more effective."

The thought of an injection under my eyelid terrified me. At the same time, it was oddly comforting to know how numb my mouth felt when my dentist used it. I didn't want to feel anything.

Dr. Lalwani carefully pulled down my lower eyelid and I could see the needle as it approached. There was a tiny pinch of pain and then it was over.

She disappeared behind me for a few minutes and then returned with a metal contraption. Its purpose became clear as she put it in place. It was an eye speculum, a tiny wire device that holds the eyelid open. The speculum wasn't particularly comfortable but knowing I didn't have to worry about blinking in the middle of the injection was at least a little comforting. When the speculum was in place, it was clear the time had arrived.

Dr. Lalwani stood to my side and slightly behind me. She carefully kept the needle out of my peripheral vision, but every nerve in my body could sense its presence.

"Okay, Chris, put your head back," she said with amazing calm and a soothing voice. I was sure she could sense the near panic in my body. My wife told me later that, through it all, my feet were pedaling like I was on a bike. I had no idea. All I could think about was the needle in her hand.

Oh please, keep it where it is. I need more time—I'm not ready yet.

"Just relax, Chris. Breathe. Breathe. Look here," she said, holding her left hand above my head and to the left.

I was paying careful attention, thinking that I had to do exactly what she told me. Not even the drill instructors in the Marine Corps got this kind of focus from me.

I didn't see her right hand or the needle, but I felt it enter my right eye. My mind was racing, and my body was frozen. It took a moment to realize there was no pain, only pressure, which provided some comfort, but I was acutely aware that the needle was still in my eye.

Keep staring where she told you to! Stay still! Don't move!

As she removed the needle, I saw a ripple in my eye, like a rock thrown into a still pond. And then all I saw was black. Nothing. But I didn't care. The needle was out. The clamp was off my eye. I could breathe again.

Before I could even ask about it, vision began to return to my eye. Within seconds things were back to the way they had been before the injection. One eye down, one to go. I was no more relaxed or comfortable when she repeated the process on my left eye, but knowing what to expect helped me keep my panic in check.

Fortunately for me, the fear of the injection was far worse than the injection itself, but the whole experience left me both emotionally and physically drained.

Dear God, please don't make me do this every month for the rest of my life!

"Are you okay baby?" Marilyn asked as we left the office.

"I need a drink" was all I could say.

On the way home, Marilyn stopped at a liquor store and bought me a special bottle of bourbon. It turned out to be a smart move. There would be months when the promise of my favorite whiskey was the only thing that got me back into Dr. Lalwani's chair.

Just days after the first injections, I began to see improvements in my vision, and less than two weeks later it returned to the way I remembered it before our honeymoon in Italy. The injections never got easier, but I knew what to expect and they were always over quickly.

About six months later, during one of my examinations, Dr. Lalwani announced that she did not see any sign of further development of those small, leaky blood vessels under my retina.

"Let's skip the injections this time."

"So, it's gone? No more wet?"

"I don't know yet. All I can tell you is I don't see any signs of it right now. Let's just see where we are next month."

Next month the results of her examination were the same. "Let's give it six weeks and see how things go, Chris."

After that it was two months and then three. With each visit, I returned to her office hoping to hear the same news, dreading the thought that this would be the visit when I learned that my eyes were no longer "dry."

Over the next several years, life seemed to return to the way it had been before our honeymoon in Sicily. Other than the visits to Dr. Lalwani's office every few months, my disease had little impact on my day-to-day life. I hadn't forgotten the facts. I still had a disease that would eventually rob me of my central vision, but that was an intellectual understanding. There was little emotion tied to it.

The cells in my macula were dying from the outside in, rather than from the center out. As a result, my field of view was slowly narrowing, but my ability to focus on the items within that field of view was unaffected. As with many people over fifty, I wore bifocals for reading, but my uncorrected distance vision, within my narrowing field of view, was 20/25, nearly normal. As a result, as a practical matter, for the first five or six years following my diagnosis, macular degeneration had little impact on my quality of life. I could still safely ride a motorcycle, every chance I got I was on the ski slopes, I drove a car, and I kept parking in the back of the parking lot.

Marilyn continued to believe in a cure. I continued to believe in Dr. Lalwani's prognosis.

Then things started to change. I started noticing that in low-contrast lighting such as a poorly lit room, I couldn't immediately recognize people I knew. I started being careful where I sat in meetings to make sure that any window or bright lighting was behind me. I stopped skiing on overcast days when there was flat lighting that masked uneven snow. Things happen fast on a motorcycle, and I began to realize I was seeing small obstructions in the road just a little bit later than I used to. That scared me. I sold the motorcycles. I stopped skiing. And after that, within a week of my sixty-first birthday, I gave up driving. That loss of independence was one of the biggest changes of my life.

Things were suddenly playing out exactly as Dr. Lalwani had told me they would, how science said they would. There was no miracle cure, no parking space in the front row after all.

I still see Dr. Lalwani every three or four months. When I walk into her office these days, I find myself hoping she will look at my retinas and say, "Chris, we need to give you an injection." The thought of a needle in my eye is still scary, but it's a treatment, a promise of improvement. That too is an illusion. Today, my vision is changing quickly. As Dr. Lalwani tells me, "You have lost so many cells in your maculas, Chris, that everyone you lose now could cause a noticeable difference in your eyesight."

My experience is no longer strictly an intellectual one. With each cell that dies I see the world differently, more than just visually. Losing your eyesight changes everything, whether you want it to or not. No matter how much time I spend studying the facts it won't change the future, and the truth is, no one really knows what that will hold for me. Dr. Lalwani can't explain to me why those tiny blood vessels stopped developing any more than she can tell me why they started in the first place. Even though it affects more than 11 million people in this country, there is still so little known about macular degeneration. Maybe today is the last day a cell in

Seeing Clearly

my macula will die. Maybe tomorrow will be the day they all die. Maybe Marilyn's parking karma isn't about finding a space in the front row. Maybe it's about being open to all possibilities and being okay with whatever you find.

3

An Unexpected Gift

My brother, Mike, was born on Christmas Day, just over seven years before me. He is my only sibling and one of the greatest influences in my life. Since the day I was born he has been beside me to celebrate every joyous moment and to help me navigate some of the most difficult. As with any two siblings, we had our share of disagreements, but I always knew that no matter what happened in my life, my brother was the one person I could count on to be by my side. That's what made the loss of our relationship so painful.

I don't have a lot of memories of him from when I was a little boy. What childhood memories I do have of my brother are little more than snapshots in my mind, indistinguishable from the pictures in the family album.

There are photos of Mike holding me as a baby, us standing in front of the house with him holding my hand, and us on the coast of Rhode Island. One of my favorites is us in front of the Leaning Tower of Pisa, while my father was stationed at the US naval base in Naples, Italy. I am clinging to my mother's leg and Mike, an awkward teenager, is casually leaning to the left, mimicking the tilt of the tower behind us.

Mike's memories of those years are more vivid than mine. One of his favorite stories to tell is of the trip home from Naples, when our father was transferred back to the States in 1966. Dad had splurged and paid the difference between what the Navy would pay and the cost of a first-class ticket on the ocean liner, the SS *Constitution*. My parents probably chose the *Constitution*, in part, because of the notoriety of the ship itself. Grace Kelly had sailed on it from New York to Monaco for her wedding to Prince Rainier. It had been featured in the movie *An Affair to Remember*, starring one of my mother's favorites, Cary Grant, as well as in several episodes of *I Love Lucy*.

Mike would have been a freshman in high school. I was in the second grade. I can imagine the instructions he must have received from Dad. "This is a very special cruise for your mother, and I don't want her having to spend the whole goddamn trip chasing after your brother. I need you to do that. That's your job, Mike. Do you understand me?"

"Yes, sir" would have been the only possible answer to that question.

According to Mike, at some point during that cruise I was driving him crazy. He'd had enough and decided to teach me a lesson. He claims that he grabbed me by my ankles and held me over the side of the ship, threatening to drop me. "They will never know, you little brat. 'Where's your brother, Mike? I don't know, Mom. He was right here.'"

I have no memory of that event except through the story he has retold over the years. I suspect it has been embellished with each telling, but it illustrates the relationship we had growing up. Mike's job was to take care of me. Mine was to torment him.

Our paternal grandfather was a tough man and a strict disciplinarian with huge expectations of his two boys. Much of my father's view of how to raise a son would have come from his father, and I can imagine that a career in the Navy, starting during World War II, would have reinforced that. Like his father, Dad was an extremely disciplined man, and like his father he expected the same of his two boys, especially Mike. Dad was particularly hard on my brother. He expected him to be tough. One of the best examples is a story I have heard my father tell countless times about one of Mike's run-ins with the school bully, always with a hint of pride.

One day, when Mike was in elementary school, a bully chased him home. When Mike got to the house he ran up on the porch where Dad was standing. "Dad! Dad! That kid is trying to beat me up!" The other kid just stood there looking at Mike and my father. I can imagine Mike's thoughts when he saw Dad standing there: *Boy, you are in trouble now. My dad is going to kick your butt!*

Dad looked at the kid, then at my brother, and said, "Who would you rather fight, me or him?" Mike looked up at Dad and then down at the school bully standing there defiant, with his hands on his hips. It only took an instant for Mike to make that choice. My brother leaped off the porch, tackling the other boy, and began slamming his head on the ground before Dad quickly broke up the fight. Dad usually ended the story with, "I thought Mike was going to kill him. I was thinking, oh shit, now I am going to have to fight this kid's old man!"

Mom was never a fan of Dad's strict views on discipline, and when I came along, she wouldn't tolerate him treating me that way. I would imagine that Mike felt it was up to him to teach me some of the same lessons he had learned from Dad. For example, when I was in the third or fourth grade, we were living in Navy housing, a short walk from the elementary school that I was attending. As I was walking home from school one day I ran into the school bully, just across the street from where we lived. He was a year older, and a year bigger than me. I have no idea what caused it, but I found myself on the ground rolling around fighting for, what seemed like, my life. I could see my brother in front of our building. As the fight broke out, he came running across the street.

Oh, thank God, I thought. *Boy, are you in trouble when my brother gets here.*

As the kid continued to clobber me, Mike bent over and yelled, "Chris, do what I told you to do! Do what I told you!"

I don't know what you told me. Please help me!

The kid rolled me over on my back, sat on my chest, and hit me square in the face. That was the last swing he took. Mike ripped him off me and threw him aside like a rag doll. "If you can't fight fair then get the hell out of here!" The kid took off and I never had an issue with him again. To this day I have no idea what I was supposed to do, but clearly Mike was trying to teach me how to defend myself, just as our father had taught him.

Even in those early years, it was evident to me that Mike and Dad were pretty tight—a relationship that would last a lifetime. I can't help but wonder if the bond between my father and brother, in at least some small part, came initially from a shared resentment toward me. Mom's protectiveness toward me stifled Dad's sense of how to teach a child discipline, and it may have led my brother to feel resentful about how strictly he was treated as a young boy. He was jealous of my "easy life."

But Dad wasn't the only influence in Mike's life. Mom was a loving woman who never had a bad word for anyone. She was raised in a more loving, nurturing environment than our father and demanded the same for her children, particularly her youngest.

Mom's loving and nurturing way not only shielded me, but it also softened my brother's hard edges that would have been forged by Dad. It was Mom's influence that led my brother to take on more of a mentor role with me, teaching me the lessons on strength he'd learned from our father and the softer, more cultured things he'd learned from Mom.

One of my most vivid memories of those years was when I was ten or eleven years old. Mike would have been seventeen or eighteen. Our father was stationed at the Bainbridge Naval Training Center in Port Deposit, Maryland, a tiny town with less than a thousand residents, located forty miles northeast of Baltimore on the eastern bank of the Susquehanna River. The base had once been a vibrant training center for sailors headed off to fight in World War II but had been fighting closure for years. The only thing left there when we arrived in 1966 was the Nuclear Power School, where they taught sailors how to operate and maintain shipboard nuclear reactors. It was a small base in the middle of nowhere, and it closed permanently soon after we left four years later.

Living in such a remote location there were few opportunities to see big-name rock bands nearby, and Mom and Dad were not the types of parents who would be open to allowing their high school-age son to drive into the big city of Baltimore, forty miles away. So, when Gary Puckett and the Union Gap announced they were going to play a show at the Navy base, only a few miles from home, Mike was excited. Gary Puckett had three top-five hits: "Woman Woman," "Young Girl," and "Lady Willpower." He begged my parents to let him go and they agreed on one condition: "You have to take Chris." I am not sure why that was a condition. While I looked up to my brother, I was still young and at times took joy in tormenting him. Maybe I asked to go because I liked the music and wanted to be like my big brother, or maybe it was just to make his life miserable. Whatever the reason, Mike had no choice. If he wanted to see Gary Puckett in concert, he had to take me with him.

I remember having a great time with Mike that evening. I think we both did. I don't remember any animosity from my brother because of being forced to take me with him. I think he appreciated the opportunity to share his love for music with me. Even now, I occasionally find a copy of "Young Girl" on Spotify and it makes me smile.

As I matured so did our relationship. There seemed to me to be a pivotal moment for us in the summer of 1983. I had graduated from college, was a second lieutenant in the Marine Corps, and was married to my first wife, Kathleen. We had a small apartment in a triplex in San Clemente, California, and Mike and his wife, coincidentally also named Marilyn, came out to visit. I remember it feeling simultaneously odd and comforting for us to be there together as adults. It was the first time I saw myself as Mike's equal, as more than just a little kid to him.

I remember Mike and I taking a six-pack of beer and walking the short distance to the beach, where we sat and talked for hours. It wasn't the first time he and I had spent time together, but somehow things were different. It was the first time I remember thinking of Mike as a friend. Our relationship matured that week and would grow even more over the years, but he would never stop being my big brother. He would never stop looking out for me.

In 1986, Kathleen and I moved to Northern Virginia, where I found a job with a large consultant firm in their cryptographic practice. We were helping the Navy with the implementation of a secure telephone system that would make it easier for military personnel to have classified conversations remotely. The year prior, my brother's career had also taken him, his wife, and their two-year-old daughter, Christy, to Northern Virginia. They were living in Herndon, only twenty miles from where Kathleen and I lived in Arlington. Living so close, we were able to see each other far more often. It was no longer just holidays at Mom's and Dad's. Kathleen and I would go to Mike's and Marilyn's house for dinner, and I would play golf with Mike on the weekends. He was a far better golfer, but he was always there with tips on how to improve my game.

When I got frustrated with my consulting job, Mike not only

encouraged me to find something better, he also helped me find one in sales, dramatically changing the trajectory of my career. And when my first marriage was ending and I was nervous about telling Mom and Dad that I was going to get a divorce, Mike insisted on joining me for the four-hour drive to Virginia Beach, where they lived, so I would not be alone when I told them the bad news. He knew that was going to be hard and he wanted to be there for me.

The only time Mike hasn't been beside me during an important time of my life was in August 1992, after he and his family moved to Texas. He was supposed to be my best man when my second wife, Holly, and I were getting married, but it took a head-on collision to keep him away. It happened maybe a week before the wedding and we almost canceled, but he encouraged us not to. Dad stood in for Mike as my best man that day. I no longer remember the words, but I remember the emotions from the toast he gave. It was surprisingly moving, and it touched me deeply. It is the only time in my life I remember my father being so openly expressive of the love and pride he felt toward me. In some strange way, it was a wonderful wedding gift from both my brother and my father that I will always cherish.

Mike was diagnosed with macular degeneration in 2008, when he was fifty-six—five years before my diagnosis. I was fifty-four when I received the same news. Like me, he'd had some previous tests many years prior that had identified some anomalies in his retina and, like me, they ultimately determined it wasn't anything to worry about. Fortunately for him, unlike me, his eyes were never "wet" so he never had to have injections, yet he would still have to face the slow but never-ending loss of central vision. Like our father, my brother isn't one to show a lot of emotion. When I asked him how he felt about the diagnosis, he played it down.

"For the longest time I just kept thinking it was the lighting in the house. I kept getting brighter and brighter lights. Eventually the power company started to question whether I was running a grow-house here," he joked.

With some prompting he finally admitted, "Yeah, I am a little scared, Chris, but it is still a long way out before I really have to worry about it. It is a slow disease and hopefully they will find a cure."

I knew nothing about macular degeneration at the time, but Mike didn't seem too worried, so I didn't worry either. We talked little about his disease in the years leading up to my diagnosis. He didn't bring it up and I rarely thought to ask. When I did, he always played it down.

Looking back now, I better understand my brother's cavalier attitude about his disease. Dry macular degeneration is a slow, insidious disease that only reveals its true impact years later. In the case of neovascular macular degeneration, the vision loss happens quickly and dramatically, as was the case for me. Fortunately, the injections restored my eyesight in a matter of weeks, but the experience of vision loss was perhaps more real and visceral for me than it was for my brother. Had my eyes remained dry like his, I too may have had a more cavalier attitude and this story may never have been written.

Mike and I talked regularly, comparing notes about our doctors' appointments, what we were experiencing, and any promising treatments that were on the horizon. The month I was diagnosed, Genentech had announced promising results from a phase II clinical trial of a potential new drug to stop the progression of dry macular degeneration. It was the most promising treatment on the horizon. When it was clear that my eyes were "dry" and I would no longer need injections, my doctor and I started talking about whether I might qualify for the clinical trial.

I called my brother to get his thoughts.

"Hey, Mike. How's it going?"

Mike's answer to that question was always the same: "Outstanding!"

"Well, good to hear nothing's changed down in Texas. I saw my eye doctor today."

"Yeah? How'd that go?"

"Okay, I guess. My left eye is doing great, pretty much back to 20/20, if I have my glasses on. I hated those damn injections. Thank God I don't have to do that anymore! Unfortunately, they did little for my right so that eye sucks."

"It's the opposite for me. My left is getting really bad, but my right seems to be doing okay."

"Between us we have two good eyes! How's your night vision these days?"

"I just don't drive at night anymore," he answered.

"I talked to Dr. Lalwani about Genentech's drug. It just passed Phase II trials. I asked her what she thought about me applying for the Phase III trials."

"What did she say?"

"She wasn't sure I was eligible since I've been treated with injections. She's going to check it out. I'm thinking about it. Would you do that? You haven't had injections so it probably wouldn't be an issue for you to get in."

"My doctor mentioned that, too. I'm not sure, Chris."

"Why? What if it could stop things from getting worse?"

"Yeah, but how would I know that I was even getting the real drug? I could drive over an hour each way every month for more than a year, to get an injection in my eye, with all that risk just to potentially get a saline solution. Besides, even if you get the drug, who says it is even effective? It just seems risky to me. Is that worth it to you?"

"I don't know. We talked about that, too. You may be right."

Five years later it was announced that the drug had failed in two separate Phase III trials involving more than two thousand patients. Genentech's promising new drug for the treatment of macular degeneration showed no better results than a placebo. I guess Mike was right. It would have been a waste of time and an unnecessary risk.

Unfortunately, there hasn't been anything else that I am aware of that has shown any near-term promise. My doctor tells me that there is promising work in gene therapy, but it will be years before there is anything close to a treatment. I will consider a clinical trial if it gets to that stage, but for now it sounds like it is wait and see.

Over the years, my brother's eyesight and mine continued to deteriorate. Mike's disease had progressed further and by the time of Genentech's announcement, he hadn't played golf, a lifelong passion of his, in years. Like me, he no longer drove. He had a hard time watching TV, and the computer seemed to be out of the question. He was almost completely dependent on his wife. He has always been there to help me navigate the challenges in my life, and he was doing it again by giving me some sense of what my future would hold.

It was about that time when I started hearing stories from Mike's wife that she was noticing unusual behavior from him. He seemed to be more forgetful. He was having difficulty coming up with simple words such as "spatula." Instead, it would become the "food flipper thing." He would occasionally forget people's names or get confused about appointments. It didn't happen all the time. Most people who saw him casually would never notice. But because Marilyn was with him almost all the time, she saw it and it worried her. It wasn't obvious to me, but I wasn't there. I only talked to him on the phone.

What was most alarming for Marilyn was his anger. Mike has always had strong opinions, but I would never have called him a bitter person. Yet he was suddenly prone to fits of anger. He would scream at her at night, telling her he hated her and that he knew she wanted him to die. The next morning, he would get up and act as if nothing had happened. Something was seriously wrong, so they saw a neurologist. The diagnosis this time was dementia or mild cognitive impairment. The news shocked me to my core. Mike has been the one constant in my life. The one person whom I have always known I could count on to be there no matter what. He is the only person in the world today who has known me my entire life. I couldn't bear the thought of him slipping away right in front of me—and it wasn't lost on me that, as with macular degeneration, the same fate might await me as well.

I called Mike to check in on him shortly after hearing the news from his wife.

"Hey, Mike. It's Chris. How are you?"

"Okay."

"Marilyn told me a little bit about your appointment with the neurologist. I am so sorry, Mike. How are you doing with all that? Sounds like a lot."

"Tell you what, Chris. For my whole life, the two things that scared me most were losing my eyesight or losing my mind. Now I am losing both."

"I know, Mike. I can't imagine how scary that must be."

Over the coming weeks we talked several times about how he was dealing with everything. I could hear in his voice that he was worried, but he has always been stoic, and he was "staying positive."

Hearing the vulnerability in my brother's voice was hard. I had never experienced that before in the nearly sixty years I had known him. No matter what, he had always been strong, confident, and positive: Mr. "Outstanding." And the worst was yet to come.

What I never saw coming was how quickly Mike's new circumstances would nearly destroy our relationship. It happened in what seemed like days.

Seeing Clearly

We grew up in a family where debate was a sport—an extreme sport at times. The first time I brought my future wife, Holly, home to meet my parents she asked, "Why does your family fight so much?"

"Fight? What are you talking about?"

"All you did was argue all night long about politics."

"Oh that. That's not arguing—that's debating. That's just what we do. In our family debating is a sport."

"Well, it felt like fighting to me."

My brother's and my political views had diverged over the last ten years. He had become a staunch right-wing conservative. He would call me a bleeding-heart liberal. Personally, I consider myself more moderate, but for my brother anything left of Rush Limbaugh is liberal. Over the years, politics have been the source of a lot of friendly debates. Rarely would a phone call between us end without a couple of potshots at the other for his political views. By the time of Mike's latest diagnosis, the debates between us had turned a lot less friendly. I finally decided I would not discuss politics with him. If he would make an off-color joke about something a Democrat did recently, I would simply laugh and say, "Ha! I bet that pissed you off." I loved my brother, but he was getting downright nasty, so I refused to take the bait.

Prior to his dementia diagnosis Mike had found a new passion for firearms and had secured a concealed weapon permit. I may be more liberal in my political beliefs than my brother, but I have no issue with responsible gun ownership. I had a lot of experience with weapons during my days in the Marine Corps. I understand the passion for firearms as a sport and, in some cases, as a form of self-defense. I just don't choose to have one myself.

To me, Mike's carrying a weapon with a diagnosis of macular degeneration was questionable. It was another thing altogether when you included dementia. I did a few Google searches and learned that in the state of Texas, remarkably, you can be completely blind and still carry a concealed weapon. But there is a specific exclusion for anyone diagnosed with dementia. Such a diagnosis prohibits you from obtaining a concealed weapon permit. I had to agree with that. The idea of someone with bad eyesight *and* dementia, who was also prone to fits of anger, walking around with a concealed and loaded weapon seemed like a recipe for disaster.

When I brought it up with him on a call, he was furious.

"Chris, my eyesight is fine. Anytime I would have to use this weapon would be inside twenty-five feet and I see fine at that distance. I would not have any issue hitting the right target."

"But Mike, what about the dementia?"

"Dementia! Are you kidding me? Where did you hear that?"

"Isn't that what the neurologist told you?"

"He said it was just typical memory problems that happen to us all as we get older. You just wait. You will see. Goddammit, I can't believe what a liberal you have turned into. You won't be happy until you take all our guns away, will you? Just like the rest of you damn Democrats."

Suddenly it was just typical age-related memory issues, not dementia.

After multiple phone calls and text messages with my sister-in-law, Marilyn, and their daughter, Christy, we all agreed that we needed to take his handguns and the best approach would be to blame it on me. "Tell him I will call the state police if he continues to carry a concealed weapon," I said. I knew the risk. He was so much like my father. When he made up his mind about something there was no changing it and he did not like being told what to do. With his temper where it was these days and his polarized political views, I was certain this would turn ugly. He would be furious with me, but I would rather it be me than Marilyn and Christy. I lived in Colorado; they had to deal with the fallout firsthand. If he never

Seeing Clearly

spoke to me again, I figured that was a worthwhile trade. Besides, how could he not get past it? We had been through so much together. Once he calmed down, he would understand. Yes, he was a lot like my father, but he also had our mother's heart. He would eventually come around.

I seriously underestimated his anger.

Marilyn and Christy eventually were successful in taking his weapons away, and for more than two years he wouldn't talk to me. My calls went to voicemail; text and email messages were ignored. Marilyn would periodically text me or call me when she had a minute alone to update me on his condition, which was getting progressively worse.

I could only guess what was going on in my brother's mind, and it broke my heart that I couldn't be there for him as he had been for me my entire life. I have some sense, based on my own experience, of how the loss of his eyesight might have been impacting him. At times I get mad, frustrated, and scared and I just want to yell, "It's not fair!" Someone must be to blame. With cognitive impairment added to the mix, I can only imagine the compounding effect.

When asked about me, Mike would tell his wife, Marilyn, that I had "ruined his life." Maybe the only way I could support him now was to let him go through this alone. I hated that, but what choice did I have.

As I saw what was happening with my brother, it was hard not to project forward in my own life. Mike was the first to be diagnosed with macular degeneration. Was dementia just around the corner for me as well? *How will it begin? What will it feel like? How will I even know it's happening to me?* Suddenly I was acutely aware of every item I misplaced and every little detail I couldn't immediately recall. *Is this dementia?* It wasn't a conscious thought at the time but, as I think back on it now, I can feel the overwhelming desire I had to run just below the surface. I wanted to run away from what was happening with my brother. I wanted to run away from the frightened future I now envisioned for myself. Most of all, I wanted to run away from the pain of all the loss I was feeling. It is what I have always done, but I didn't understand that at the time. All I could articulate was that whatever the future held for me, I didn't want to experience the anger that my brother was experiencing. My wife, Marilyn, didn't deserve that. I remember thinking, *If that's what I have to look forward to, I better get some help.* That was a decision that would dramatically change my life.

4

A New Language

In the summer of 2019, shortly after the falling out with my brother, I started researching therapists in the area. I had worked with a therapist, Brent, for more than a year following my divorce from Holly, but it had been seven years since I had seen him, and he had moved to California. We had made a lot of progress in our work together, and as I began to look for a new therapist, I saw it as strictly a precautionary action.

"I think it would be good to find someone I can have a relationship with just in case things get worse," I told my wife, Marilyn. The situation with Mike had unsettled me, and I had what I could only describe as a "low-grade fever." Something was bothering me, but I couldn't clearly articulate what it was. I eventually narrowed my list of potential therapists to four. One never returned my call and another was ridiculously expensive. I saw the third one, who was right down the street from my home, and I could tell from the moment I walked in that there was no chemistry. I almost gave up, but there was one more on the list whom I had discounted initially because he seemed a bit too spiritual to me. I figured what the hell, why not give him a call just to see? After a brief conversation we scheduled an introductory session.

Chad's office was about ten miles from my home in Boulder. On my first appointment, he met me in the lobby. "You must be Chris. I'm Chad."

"Yes, great to meet you, Chad."

"You can leave your shoes here." He was barefoot, an indication of his other calling as a Zen priest, I guessed.

His office was small, with just enough room for two upholstered chairs. No couples therapy, I assumed. As we entered the room, he said, "Have a seat," not pointing to either seat or taking one himself. *Perhaps this is the first test,* I thought. *Should I sit by the door ready to run or the back corner where I am committed?* I chose the latter and sat in the back. Seeing a therapist in the first place was purely preventative. As far as I was concerned, I did not have any huge emotional issues.

I immediately liked Chad. He was easy to talk to, he listened, and he challenged me with comments such as, "I didn't ask you what you thought. I asked you how you felt." I liked that. We spent the first few sessions getting to know each other, laying out the basic building blocks for our work together. On about the third visit, I said to him, "It's strange. In so many ways I feel more confident and self-assured today than I have at any point in my life. I have had friends, colleagues, and customers describe me as unflappable or confident, and at times I can clearly see that in me."

"What's wrong with that?"

"Nothing. But the funny thing is, that may be how I look on the outside, but all too often the thought running through my head is, *Dear God, is today the day they figure out that I am a fake, that I am in way over my head?* How can both of those things be true, Chad? I hate that part of me. How do I get rid of that?"

"What does it feel like to you when you get that feeling, that you aren't good enough?"

Seeing Clearly

"I don't know. I guess it feels like shit."

"Okay, but how does feeling like shit feel?"

"I don't know. I guess I want it to stop. I just don't understand why I still struggle with confidence. I mean, if I look around, I can see so many reasons why I should feel confident. Particularly at work. I am pretty good at what I do. Why the hell do I feel this way?"

"You are smart, Chris. Very smart. That's your problem. As with any skill, if you overuse it, it can become a liability. You can't think your way through this. You have to learn to feel your way through. Are you willing to try something, Chris?"

Feel my way? What the hell does that mean?

"Uh, I guess so," I answered.

"Great! Close your eyes."

I sat back and closed my eyes.

"I want you to focus on a time when you felt that you weren't good enough. Don't push the feeling away. Move toward it. Just let it wash over you."

I sat there with my eyes closed trying to somehow mentally levitate toward some unknown feeling. *This feels crazy but what the hell. That's why I am here...*

"Tell me what you feel, Chris."

"I guess it is fear," I answered.

"Fear. Good. What does that look like? Describe it to me."

"What does it look like? I don't know. Fear. I'm scared, I guess."

"Try to picture that fear. What does it look like? Is it dark, is it smoky? Describe it to me."

"I don't know, I can't really see it. It's kind of everywhere. I mean it is kind of like asking a fish to describe water. It just surrounds me. I guess it is like how a scared little boy must feel."

Where the hell is he going with this?

"A small child. Wonderful! Like how old you think?"

"Five, six?"

"Okay. Great. So, I want you to picture that scared little boy. Can you see him?"

"I guess. Okay. Yes. I can see him. I don't like him, but I can see him."

"You don't like him—why?"

"Because he is that part of me that I hate the most. The part I really want to get rid of."

"But Chris, he is just a little boy, and he is scared. Do you want to just yell at him and tell him to get away from you? Is that what you would do if you saw him sitting there afraid?"

"Well, no, of course not." Suddenly I felt tears welling up in my eyes. "No, never. I would never do that!"

"Then what would you say to him, Chris?"

I sat and thought about it for a moment before answering. "I guess I would ask him what he is afraid of. And I would listen and help him see that everything is going to be okay. He doesn't need to be afraid."

"Of course you would. So, let me ask you something. Why can't you be that compassionate to yourself? Because you know what, Chris? That little boy is a part of you, and you can't hide him or ignore him. You have to learn to love him, to comfort him. Allow him to express his fears, because if you don't, as with any five-year-old, he will make sure his voice is heard by acting out."

As we sat and talked about it more I began to understand. That little boy had been inside me my entire life. I could see him as I looked back at that picture in front of the Leaning Tower of Pisa with my brother as I desperately clung to my mother's leg. I saw him as a teenager, in his shy, introverted behavior, afraid to ask the girl he liked to dance, and I began to get a glimpse of his presence during my late forties following the death of my parents. Before our divorce, my ex-wife, Holly, said to me, "I don't think you have ever truly grieved the loss of your mother."

Seeing Clearly

"Not true," I responded. "I've grieved. I just don't see a reason to wallow in self-pity. What use is that?"

Then my father died, and I grieved even less.

How frightened that little boy inside me must have been. For so many years I ignored him, or worse, I literally told him to shut up. What Chad was helping me see for the first time was the role that unrecognized or repressed emotions had played in my life. He was helping me see that the little boy was still there, and he was still scared—and there was plenty of reason for him to be even more fearful now.

In one of our sessions, Chad asked me if I was afraid about losing my eyesight.

"No," I said. "People ask me that a lot and it seems like I should be, but no matter how hard I try to feel the fear, it just isn't there."

"Okay. That's possible," he said. "Then what do you feel when you think about what's happening with your eyesight?"

I sat and thought about that for a minute, trying to understand my feelings, and suddenly it came to me. "I feel loss." And with that realization came a flood of emotions.

Losing my central vision isn't the hardest part. Seeing the world around me become hazy and unfocused is unquestionably a loss, but what is far more difficult for me is the loss of independence that it brings. It can be infuriating. I feel so capable, and yet little things that I have always taken for granted have become monumental feats, if not impossible. It wasn't obvious to me at the time, but today I see clearly how that makes me feel less capable—weak—and for a guy who was raised as I was, that is frightening.

Pain is not necessarily a bad thing. It is a message that something is wrong—pay attention. Just like it would be very harmful to ignore the pain you feel when you mistakenly touch something very hot, ignoring an equally "hot" emotion can be devastating.

My ex-wife was right, I never really grieved the loss of my

mother. Every time I got even a glimpse of the pain that lay below the surface following her death I did everything I could to ignore it and look the other way. It was the emotional equivalent of leaving my hand on a hot stove. It is impossible for me to say for sure what role that played in the events that ultimately ended our marriage, but I have little doubt that it was at least a factor.

As I worked with Chad, I began to see the signs of a growing fear in my daily life. It's the little things that help shine a light on what is just below the surface. Like when I am riding with my wife in the car and we hit an unexpected bump. *Damn it! How fast are you driving?* is my first thought. Or when I open the refrigerator to get the mayonnaise out for a sandwich, but I can't find it. *Who the hell moved the mayo?*

The truth is, she wasn't going too fast, and the mayonnaise was in the back where it always was; I just couldn't see it. My anger was almost certainly rooted in my fear of vulnerability—in my fear of feeling weak. I didn't see that bump and it startled me, and when I couldn't find something so simple as a jar of mayonnaise it served as another reminder of all the things I would no longer be able to do myself and of my growing dependence on others. All I could feel was my growing "weakness."

I have always been solution oriented. When I see a problem, I want to fix it and I want to do it in the most expedient fashion. It is something that has caused more than a little tension in many of my romantic relationships. The feedback is usually something like, "Why do you always feel the need to solve every problem? Why can't you just listen sometimes?" I suspect it has a lot to do with my discomfort with painful emotions. I would rather try to get to the root of the problem instead of taking time to experience the emotion, but Chad would have none of that with me. If something he and I were discussing triggered a strong emotion, I would jump right to trying to explain why I felt that way—or sometimes I would just make a joke in an effort to diffuse what I was feeling. When I did, Chad would interrupt me in mid-sentence. "Chris, wait! This is important. Stop and let yourself feel that. Just take a moment and experience it." He forced me to sit and experience my emotions time after time. It was excruciating for a guy who spent most of his life dodging emotions.

"It is just frustrating, Chad. I spent so much time in therapy following my divorce trying to figure myself out and I felt like I learned a lot, but the more time I spend with you the more it seems like a huge ball of yarn that I can never unravel. I see little bits of information, and every time I pull on one of the strings, I find it isn't connected to what I thought it was. How do I fix this? I am tired of feeling afraid."

Chad laughed. "Chris, I am sorry to tell you this, but you can't 'fix' this. If you spend the rest of your life looking inside trying to understand your emotions, maybe you will be able to unravel ten percent of that ball of yarn. You will never unravel it all. I know how uncomfortable that makes you feel."

"It does, Chad. It just feels like the more I learn about myself, the more I realize how little I know. It's just not how I am wired."

"You know what the great news is, Chris?"

"No, what? Please tell me!"

"You may never be able to completely unravel that ball of yarn, but maybe, for the first time in your life, you are beginning to see that it exists. You can't think your way through this. The only way is to feel it, and that is what you need to learn: the language of emotions."

As an engineer I am a left-brained, linear thinker. Learning a new language should be easy for me. They tend to be very structured, with clear patterns. Right down my alley. But the language Chad was trying to teach me made little sense. The language of emotions, for me, follows no discernible pattern. I knew that he was right. I had to learn how to open my heart and feel my way through because, just as if I were dropped off alone in a foreign country, learning the language was essential for my survival. As my disease progresses, there will be countless new ways for me to be fearful, like things I can trip over in the dark or simply getting lost on the way back from the restroom in an unfamiliar restaurant. Looking back I can see how my ignorance of the language of emotions has played a role in some of the darkest times of my life.

One of the most painful was a fight I had with my father just months before he died.

Mom had died a couple years prior, and Dad was living alone in an independent senior facility near my brother in Texas. Mike started noticing dents in Dad's car. When asked about it, Dad would say a shopping cart had hit his car, or that another careless driver had slammed their door into his. Mike began to casually check Dad's car whenever he saw him and, miraculously, the old dents would disappear and a new one would show up each time.

By coincidence, Mike and Dad drove the exact same model and color car: a red Buick LaCrosse. One day Mike took his car to a nearby body shop to have a small dent repaired, and when the guy saw the car and heard Mike's name he asked, "Are you any relation to Alfred Monnette?"

"Yeah! He's my father. How do you know him?"

"At first, I thought you were bringing in his car for repair. He has been here a number of times in the last few months to have dents repaired."

As Mike started to pay more attention to Dad's driving, it didn't take long for him to realize just how dangerous he had become. Dad really shouldn't have been driving at all. Mike was afraid he might kill himself or someone else. Mike and I talked about it and agreed—Dad really didn't need a car. Mike lived just around the corner from Dad, and it would be easy for Mike or his wife to drive

Seeing Clearly

Dad anywhere he needed to go. Mike tried to broach the subject with Dad, but Dad wouldn't even discuss it. There was no way he was giving up his car voluntarily, so we did the only thing we could do for his safety and the safety of others: We stole it from him.

I have made a lot of mistakes in my life that I would love to have back, but few as big as what happened after taking Dad's car. I was living in Oregon at the time and flew down to Texas to talk to him, to try and smooth things over between us. Shortly after I arrived, Mike drove me over to see Dad. We knocked on the door to his room.

"Hi, Dad," I said as he opened the door.

"What the hell are you doing here?" he said as he tried to slam the door in our faces.

I jammed my foot in the door to keep it from closing. "Dad, we need to talk." I followed him into his apartment.

Mike knew where this was going and wanted none of it. He had been dealing with Dad's anger over the loss of his car for weeks now.

"Chris, give me a call when you need a ride. I am going home," he said, and left.

How I wish I would have left with him.

"Get the hell out of here," Dad snarled at me. "This is my place, and you aren't welcome here."

"No, I won't. I flew all the way from Oregon to talk to you and I am not leaving until we do. Dad, you are being unreasonable."

He stormed past me, nearly pushing me over, and walked out the door and down the hallway. Dad wasn't a small man, and even in his eighties he had a presence much greater than his six-foot-two frame. I had always loved and respected my father but there was always a little fear as well. He could be intimidating, and as kids Mike and I had learned that his word was final. Challenging him would never end well. But he and I had become close after Mom's passing and I thought that if we could just talk, he would understand.

"Come on, Dad. Please stop. I really want to talk to you."

I followed him into the kitchen of the community dining room where the staff was preparing for the next meal.

When one of the staff members saw us walk into the kitchen she said, "Well hello there, Mr. Monnette. Who is this young man with you? Is this your son?"

"Who, him? I have no idea. I think he just got out of prison or something."

"Oh, come on, Mr. Monnette, he looks just like you. He is your son, isn't he?"

Finding no support there, Dad stormed out the door back into the hallway.

"Dad!" I pleaded.

He kept walking. We turned a corner and entered a small sitting area where two hallways joined. That's when something came over me. I just couldn't take it. He wasn't just being unreasonable; he was being mean and nasty.

I grabbed him by the arm to stop him and he spun around, and for an instant I was sure he was going to punch me in the face. Before he could, I grabbed both of his arms and yelled, "Dad, we are going to talk whether you like it or not!"

"God damn it, I used to change your diapers! Don't you ever try to tell me what to do! I am the father. You are just some snot-nose kid!" He tried to wrestle free from my grip, but he was eighty-one and I was forty-eight. I slammed him against the wall and looked him straight in the eyes.

"Listen, old man. I don't have to take that shit from you, not anymore! I am stronger than you and I can take you down. I am not afraid of you."

He knew I was right. He could no longer take me in a physical fight, and suddenly I too realized that there was no way he would ever give in, not Master Chief Monnette. As the futility of my

Seeing Clearly

actions began to sink in, I let him go. He had won. He always did. I could physically overpower him, but I could never beat him in a war of wills. When we were kids, he used to say, "You may get bigger than me, but you will never be meaner than me." I'd always thought that was a joke, but I learned that day just how serious he was.

I looked at him one last time with contempt in my eyes. There was no sorrow, no remorse, and certainly no love. I turned and walked out. By the grace of God, I have no clear memory of my last words to him that day. I imagine they were something like, "To hell with you, old man." Or simply, "Fuck you."

I have no idea what he did after I turned my back on him and walked out. He would have been furious. No one treated my father that way, especially not one of his sons, particularly his youngest. To this day I am surprised he didn't pick up a book or a lamp and throw it at the back of my head as I walked away. He was not a violent man and had never done anything like that before, but I had pushed him farther than I had ever seen anyone push him. I would like to think that there was something deep inside Dad that reminded him that I was his son and that he loved me, but I think, at least for that moment, he might have been afraid of me. To this day, that thought breaks my heart.

That was the last conversation I had with my father. Just a few months later, on his eighty-second birthday, he slipped and fell while getting out of Mike's car and hit his head on the pavement. The next time I saw him he was in a nursing home, almost completely unresponsive, just weeks before he died.

It was my work with Chad that helped me begin to understand what had happened that day. Neither my father nor I had any fluency in the language of emotions, and it is easy to look back now and see what went wrong. Sure, I was frustrated that he wouldn't talk to me. I had flown two thousand miles to see him, and he would not even give me the time of day. I was hurt, but that wasn't the emotion that caused such a dramatic reaction. It was fear. Mom had just died two years before, and I could see in my father a fragility I had never seen in him before. I was frightened that I was going to lose him too. I knew it was coming. I just wasn't ready. After Mom's passing, Dad and I had become very close. I wasn't ready to lose him. Not yet. I was frightened, but at the time I couldn't identify that. All I could feel was anger. Someone had to be to blame, and he gave me plenty of reason to blame him that day rather than to look inside at what I was really feeling.

Deep inside, my father was likely frightened as well. He had watched his wife of nearly sixty years slip away right before his eyes and he couldn't stop it. Now, his two sons were telling him he too was reaching the end by taking away his car: a huge sign of independence. I doubt it was a conscious thought that day, but I would bet that not too far below the surface he too knew the end was in sight. And like me, he too would not have been able to identify that the emotion he was feeling was fear.

So, there we were, two grown men who cared deeply for each other, scared to death, and all we could do was fight. How I wish I would have just hugged him and said, "Dad, I'm afraid too."

Thirteen years later, as I was turning only sixty-one, I too was forced to give up driving. Unlike my father, the decision was mine. My eyesight was getting too bad to be behind the wheel. While the decision was all mine, the loss of independence was no less real than my father's. To this day, I still struggle with telling people that I no longer drive. Somewhere inside I feel as though I will be judged poorly because of my disability. I won't ask for help. I'll just call an Uber and not mention the reason. Maintaining that charade probably isn't a big deal.

But what if the stakes were raised and what was at risk was more than just a little embarrassment about my inability to drive? What if I could rewind the clock to the last conversation I would ever have

Seeing Clearly

with my father? Would it be worth being vulnerable and telling him how afraid I was? Would it be worth telling him how much I loved him and hated what was happening?

Or, what if what was at risk was my marriage? Would it be worth it to me to let my wife and children see me openly express the nearly crippling pain I felt from the death of my mother? Would it be worth the embarrassment to say I need help; I can't carry this burden alone?

Today, I can say with absolute certainty that had I understood the emotional undercurrent that was distorting my view of things at those times in my life I would have done almost anything to prevent what happened. I can say with equal conviction that I will do anything I can to prevent anything like that happening again.

5

Lucky Thirteen

There are many people who grew up in families who talked about their emotions. I wasn't one of them. In fact, I would say quite the opposite. Sure, Mom would tell us how much she loved us, or Dad might express his anger about something, but none of us talked about the feelings themselves. That level of vulnerability just didn't exist, particularly with my father.

My mother grew up in a white-collar family of four children: three girls and one boy. Her father, Julius Pachor, was a self-made man who came to the United States from Austria-Hungary as a young merchant marine at the age of seventeen. He eventually reached the executive ranks with a large US corporation, allowing him to provide a comfortable life for his family.

Dad's family was from the other side of the tracks. Life was much harder for them than it was for my mother's family. He was born in 1925 just before the Great Depression, the youngest of two boys. Times were tough, and his father instilled strict discipline in his children. As a young boy, if Dad didn't get home before the streetlights came on, his punishment might be to kneel on the hardwood floors for an hour holding a Bible in each outstretched

Seeing Clearly

arm. As a teenager he once asked his father if he could buy a car if he saved up enough money. His father agreed and Dad saved every dime he could through selling papers and odd jobs until he had enough to buy a car. When he did, his father took it from him; it was now the family car. "I said you could buy it; I never said you could drive it." It was a tough lesson to learn as a young man. Times were tough, and everyone had to do what needed to be done to help the family survive.

Dad's older brother, Herbert, enlisted in the US Navy in March 1941. He must've lied about his age as he would not turn eighteen until October of that year, but for some unknown reason he couldn't wait. We were at war, and I imagine he felt compelled to join the fight.

In late July or early August of the following year, Herbert came home to Toledo to visit his family. His younger brother, Bud, my dad, would have been there to greet him. I imagine how proud he must have been of his older brother, Seaman First Class Monnett. (They were still using the original spelling of our family name, without the *e* on the end, before it was later added as the result of some unknown fallout between my grandfather and his siblings.)

Herbert was out defending the country, fighting Nazis. I don't know if the purpose of Herbert's visit was a send-off for my father, who had just enlisted in the Navy as well, or if the visit was the catalyst for my father's decision to enlist. Either way, like his older brother, Dad lied about his age and enlisted in the US Navy on August 18, 1942, seven months before his eighteenth birthday.

Dad was a patriotic man, and I always knew him to have a strong sense of duty. The Japanese had just attacked Pearl Harbor in December, and the pull to join his brother in the fight must have been tremendous.

Shortly after Herbert's visit, Dad was shipped off to boot camp at the Naval Training Center in Great Lakes, Illinois. He could not have been there more than a few days when his father received the following telegram:

WASHINGTON DC AUG 25 1046P
ALFRED ALEXANDER MONNETT
1105 MIAMI ST (TOLEDO OHIO)

THE NAVY DEPARTMENT DEEPLY REGRETS TO INFORM YOU THAT YOUR SON HERBERT ROLLAND MONNETT SEAMAN FIRST CLASS US NAVY IS MISSING IN THE PERFORMANCE OF HIS DUTY AND IN THE SERVICE OF HIS COUNTRY THE DEPARTMENT APPRECIATES YOUR GREAT ANXIETY BUT DETAILS NOT NOW AVAILABLE AND DELAY IN RECEIPT THEREOF MUST NECESSARILY BE EXPECTED TO PREVENT POSSIBLE AID TO OUR ENEMIES PLEASE DO NOT DIVULGE THE NAME OF HIS SHIP OR STATION
REAR ADMIRAL RANDALL JACOBS CHIEF OF NAVAL PERSONNEL

Herbert's ship, the destroyer USS *Ingram*, had been operating in the North Atlantic off the coast of Canada. They were chasing a German submarine and were in heavy fog. They collided with an oil tanker, almost five times their size. The collision set off the depth charges on the back of the ship. It sank in twenty-five seconds. Only eleven of the crew of 175 survived. Herbert was not one of them.

I cannot imagine how my father must have felt when he heard the news that day in bootcamp. As a former Marine myself, I can picture the environment. He would have been surrounded by other recruits and drill instructors, all men. The unwritten rule would have been to be strong, and no doubt, Dad's father had well prepared him for that. If there were tears, I would bet that it was only in the quiet of the night in his bunkbed, his face buried in a pillow.

Seeing Clearly

He could not let the other sailors see him be weak and vulnerable. They were at war, after all.

I don't know if there was a funeral. Herbert's body was almost certainly never recovered. Dad probably had the opportunity to go home for a day or two to be with his parents, but there was little time for grieving. Only a month later he was at the naval station in Puerto Rico. He was in the Navy now and life moved on quickly for him.

Twenty-eight years later, on August 20, 1971, just five days before the anniversary of Uncle Herbert's death, my grandfather died suddenly. Dad went to Michigan for the funeral. I don't think my mother joined him, nor did my brother or me. The stated reason was probably that we had school, or it was too expensive for us all to go. My guess is that Dad went by himself because he knew it would be a difficult, emotional event and the last thing he needed was his family there to witness any emotions. It was his job to be strong. I am sure his father would have expected as much.

Following her husband's death, my grandmother, Edith Perkins, came to live with us in Yorktown, Virginia. She was seventy-six years old and was apparently suffering from some form of dementia. I barely remember her. She was there for such a short period of time. As I recall the story, she started saying to my father things such as, "Bud, who is this strange woman in the house?"—referring to my mother. Before I knew it, she was gone. Moved to a nursing home somewhere in Newport News. If we visited her, I have not a single memory of it. I was twelve.

Years passed without a mention of my grandmother. My parents didn't talk about her around me and I never asked. I am my father's son, after all. By the time I was in my late twenties or early thirties I was certain she had died, but I didn't know how to bring it up with my father for the first time in so many years. How do you say, "By the way, Dad, is your mother still alive?" without sounding horrible.

I finally asked my mother, "Mom, what happened to grandma?"

"She passed away several years ago."

"What happened?" I asked.

"Oh dear, she was just old."

She died on August 1, 1983, when she was eighty-eight years old, twelve years after she was moved into the long-term care facility. I was twenty-four. In all that time there was never a mention of it, or if there was I have not a single memory. I know I did not attend a memorial of any kind. As with her husband, my grandfather, to this day I do not know if she is buried or if she was cremated. I imagine they were both cremated. The expense of a burial isn't something that Dad would have been comfortable with. Besides, I wonder if a cremation was just more final. A gravesite could have brought up painful memories that he might feel obligated to visit. I have no idea what became of their ashes. I am sure they were quietly and discretely spread somewhere, out of sight of anyone.

I don't know what happened the day my grandmother died, but knowing my father, I can guess. I imagine him in bed, asleep, when his phone rang at 2 a.m. one night.

"Hello?"

"Mr. Monnette?"

"Yes?"

"I am the nurse on duty at the Newport News Nursing Home."

"Yes?"

"I am sorry to tell you, but your mother passed away this evening."

After a long pause. "Okay. What do you need me to do?"

"Have you made arrangements with a funeral home."

"No. Can you recommend one?"

"Yes. There is one nearby that we work with. Would you like us to call them?"

"Yes, I appreciate that."

"Okay, we will give them a call."

Seeing Clearly

Not a tear. No time for that. There were arrangements to be made, work to be done.

My father was a master in the art of suppressing painful emotions. Like me, his earliest lessons probably began with the strict discipline that his father showed toward his boys. It was undoubtedly reinforced by the death of his brother while he was in boot camp. And it may have been finally cast in stone years later with the way I entered the world. That story begins just before the end of World War II.

In February 1943, Dad was transferred from the naval station in Puerto Rico back to the United States to attend a three-month training program at the Pre-Midshipman School located in Asbury Park, New Jersey, before heading out to sea for a two-year deployment. Just two weeks before leaving Asbury Park he met Julie Pachor, who was part of the Navy's Women's Reserve program, better known as WAVES, or Women Accepted for Volunteer Emergency Service.

It was love at first sight. They were inseparable for those two weeks, and when Dad shipped out, he promised to return to New Jersey.

In May 1943 Dad reported for duty on board LCI(L)-1002, for what would be a nearly three-year tour of duty. The ship was one of more than nine hundred landing craft designed to transport up to two hundred troops from a rear base and land them directly on a beach. They were small ships, only 158 feet in length and twenty-three feet wide, and carried a permanent crew of only twenty-eight men. The ship was so small that I don't believe it even had a name, only the hull number, LCI-1002.

During his three years at sea, Dad wrote constantly to Julie and, true to his word, in March 1946 he returned to New Jersey and got out of the Navy. They were married four months later, on July 6, 1946.

Mom's sister, my Aunt Norma, was the youngest of four children and only a year younger than my mother. As the two youngest girls they were particularly close. Like her older sister, Norma had married a military man that same year. Norma and her husband, Jimmy Ferguson, lived near Mom and Dad on the Jersey Shore. The four of them were inseparable. They spent time on the beach. They loved music, they danced, and they drank. They drank a lot, particularly Dad and my Uncle Jimmy.

I have so many memories of Mom talking about how much she wanted to have a large family. She always loved being around little babies and frequently told us how much she loved the whole experience of being pregnant. I have no memories of my father talking about his expectations for a family. Knowing a little bit about his childhood, I don't imagine him aspiring to more than a couple of kids. I can see him as being a bit more pragmatic about it. Raising a child is expensive, and a large family is very expensive. But Dad would not have had the final word on that. Dad had a humorous way of describing his relationship with his wife. "I have your mother right where she wants me," he would joke.

Anyone who knew them knew it was no joke. When it came to matters of significant importance, we all knew who pulled the strings. Dad could roar louder than anyone, but he adored his wife and when she put her foot down, nine times out of ten, things went her way. She was always very careful when she played that card, though. She was very aware of allowing her husband to be the "man of the house." When it came to how many children they would have, there is little doubt she would have called the shots.

My brother was born on Christmas Day 1951. The family photo album has pictures of their tiny home filled with toys, baby blankets, and a crib. There are photos of Dad holding his newborn son proudly. There is little doubt about how excited he was to have a son, the only one to carry on his branch of the Monnette family tree. I can imagine my father thinking he would make sure his son

Seeing Clearly

would have a better life than he had as a child. He would teach him how to be strong, to be a man. There are lots of pictures over the years in the family photo album of Mike on various sports teams—baseball, basketball. Photos of Mike standing next to his teammates in uniform smiling for a team photo. Their coach, my father, standing next to the team with a stern, serious face. Being a man was serious business.

One day, when I was probably in my late twenties, I asked Mom why they had waited so long to have a second child.

"Oh, we tried, dear, but I had a number of miscarriages. It just took that long for us to have you and you were worth the wait," she said with a loving smile.

"I didn't know that. You had more than one?"

"Oh my gosh, yes. I had twelve."

I honestly cannot remember my response. I imagine it was little more than an acknowledgment. I would not have known what to say. Twelve pregnancies, twelve lost babies! It is hard for me to imagine the emotional toll all that loss took on both of my parents. How I wish I would have pulled up a chair next to her and said, "Oh my God, Mom. I am so sorry. That must have been so hard. How did you guys get through that?" That discussion may have changed the course of my life, but I let it slip away. I have little doubt my mother would have told me the entire story had I asked, but I didn't, and she let it go. There was a lot of pain tied to those years, more than I could realize at the time, and we just didn't talk about things such as that in our family. Instead, I have had to piece what happened together from researching family timelines, Dad's military record, and family stories.

In 1955, when my Aunt Norma learned she was pregnant with her fourth child, Uncle Jimmy's drinking had become an issue and Aunt Norma was worried about bringing another baby into the troubled marriage. Norma knew of her sister's challenges with having a second baby and thought perhaps there was a solution to both of their problems. What if her sister, my mother, adopted her baby? Mom was thrilled. She would have the second child she so desperately wanted, and her sister's child would remain in the family. I am not sure when things changed, but in the end Norma could not give up her baby and my cousin Patti was born on January 13, 1956.

I have heard my father tell the story of what happened next, or at least a part of the story, countless times over the years. He had been working for the telephone company since leaving the Navy in 1946. He had been there for about ten years when he went to Philadelphia for the day to do an installation. While he was there, he saw a sign advertising a free physical examination at the Navy shipyard. "It had been a long time since I'd had a checkup, so I figured, what the hell. Afterward, I had to call your mother and tell her I had re-enlisted in the Navy. She was furious!" He always added, "I know the exact date because it was your birthday." He spent the next eighteen months at sea on the USS *Joseph P. Kennedy*.

It was only as I was writing this story that all the pieces came together. I was born on January 13, 1959, three years to the day after my cousin Patti, and three years to the day after my father re-enlisted in the Navy. Dad wasn't entirely forthcoming when he said that he reenlisted on my birthday. It was actually three years earlier, on my cousin Patti's birthday.

I will never know for certain what happened that day in Philadelphia, but I can make an educated guess. I can imagine my parents' mixed emotions. They would have been happy to hear the joyful news of Patti's birth. It would have also served as another reminder of all the failed attempts they'd had at having a second child, including potentially adopting Patti herself. Perhaps there were tears, maybe an argument. For my father, I am not sure which would have been more painful: the loss he felt himself or the loss

Seeing Clearly

that he knew he would see in the eyes of the woman he adored when he came home that evening. They both would have been difficult for him to handle. So, he re-enlisted in the Navy. In other words, he ran. It was far easier than facing the pain that awaited him at home. That is unfortunately just too familiar to me. Fifty years later I would do the same, but with far greater consequences.

It is an interesting coincidence that I was born on the thirteenth day of the month, just like Patti, who could have been my adopted sister, and it was also in my parents' thirteenth year of marriage. It is only recently that I realized just how lucky the number is to me. My parents' marriage could have ended when my dad ran off to sea, but instead he came back and they tried a thirteenth time to have another baby, this time successfully. Lucky me!

I have always tried to model the strength that I saw in my father. In many ways he had tremendous strength, but when things got tough, he is the one who ran. The fact that I am lucky enough to be here today is almost certainly a testament to the quiet strength of my mother. Knowing my mother, I can only imagine the tears she shed with each loss. It would have been devastating to her and she would not have been willing or able to keep all that pain bottled up inside as I would bet my father did. Maybe that is what gave her the emotional reserves she needed to hold their family together through such a difficult time. I would guess that it was her strength, not his, that kept them together long enough for me to even be conceived. I can see clearly now why my father loved her so dearly. I believe that she was truly the source of any real strength he had.

All of this helps me understand the environment I entered when I was born seventeen months after my father returned from his tour of duty on board the USS *Kennedy*. Twelve miscarries and a husband who ran away so he didn't have to face the pain. I can only imagine how guarded my parents, Mom in particular, must have felt when they learned she was pregnant for the thirteenth time after

Mike was born. Perhaps this would be the one, and yet, why would this one be any different? What if it wasn't? Would he run again? Would their marriage be over just like Norma and Jimmy's? With each passing day, I imagine them becoming more hopeful and yet more afraid. "What if we lose the baby now? Dear God, not now!"

When I was born, I imagine my mother clinging to me as tightly as she could, just a little tighter than she did with my older brother. It's not that she loved me more; it's just that the joy she felt was so much greater after so much pain. It also explains why she was so protective of me, why she would not tolerate the harsh discipline that my father had shown my brother. I get the sense that it also created distance between the two of them, or at least reinforced what was already there following his abrupt re-enlistment.

I can only speculate about what happened between my parents in the years surrounding my birth. I know there were some very tough times in their relationship, but they were private people and never shared any of the details. All I know is that decades later, shortly after my mother died, my father told me for the first time that he had been once "tempted" by another woman. As he told me the story, I was able to put the timeline together. It happened somewhere in that same time period.

The timing makes sense to me. There was likely an absence of joy in my father's life, which would have created a yearning for it. It may not have been something he was conscious of, not too dissimilar from the low-grade fever that brought me to Chad. Then someone came along offering the promise to fill that hole, to make him feel better. The attraction would have been strong. I am pretty sure I know what was happening with my father at the time because I have lived it myself. In my case, I was more than tempted.

My father was a flawed man, which is to say he was human. He was also a great father whom I love and miss terribly. He wasn't perfect—who is?—but my father tried hard to be the best man that he could be. Maybe his biggest flaw was he tried too hard to carry the weight of the world for the ones he loved, and he never knew when it was too much to handle by himself. He didn't know how to tell his wife that he too was overcome with grief no more than I did after he and my mother died.

It wasn't until the death of his wife after fifty-nine years of marriage that my father experienced a grief so overwhelming that he could not control it. He would break down and sob. Even today, as I write these words, my eyes are filled with tears just remembering his unimaginable sorrow.

It all started with a call. It was about 2 a.m. on January 21, 2005, twenty-two years after my grandmother had died. I was sound asleep when my phone rang.

I instinctively knew before I answered the call what had happened. "Hello."

"Mr. Monnette?"

"Yes?"

"I am the nurse on duty at Valley West Nursing Home."

"Yes?"

"I am sorry to tell you, but your mother passed away this evening."

I searched for the right thing to say and found nothing. After a long pause, "Umm. Okay. What do you need me to do?"

"Have you made prior arrangements with a funeral home?"

"We can use Musgrove Family Mortuary. They are family friends."

"Okay, Mr. Monnette. We will make arrangements with them."

"Okay, thank you."

The call was not a surprise. We had been expecting it, but I felt a finality in her words that I had never anticipated. I was numb and I found comfort in that. I knew that if I allowed even a single tear it would consume me, and I didn't have time for that. There was suddenly a lot to be done and that provided an escape from the torrent of emotions I could feel screaming for my attention.

Christopher T. Monnette

There is little doubt that my ex-wife, Holly, was right. I never allowed myself to truly grieve the loss of my mother. The truth is it was something I was unable to do. I didn't know how. Every time I felt the pain and the tears start to well up in my eyes, I looked away, changed the subject, moved on. It hurt too much, and I couldn't deal with it. I needed help but wouldn't ask. Like my father, I just wasn't wired that way.

6

Italian Driving

WHILE MY FATHER DID NOT have the best access to his emotions, that certainly didn't make him a bad person or a poor parent. He was neither. In fact, I feel fortunate to have had a father like him. Some of my own traits that I am most proud of I can directly trace to my father.

As I look back on what I know about his childhood and his early adult years, it is not a surprise that his emotional intelligence was as stifled as it was. We are, after all, products of our environment. While my earliest understanding of what it meant to be a man was heavily influenced by what I observed in my father as a young boy, that understanding was reinforced and hardened by my own experiences over the years. It wouldn't be until I was literally forced to see the world differently that I would start to understand just how much my own life conspired to leave me with little more access to my emotions than my father.

The month I turned two years old, my father was assigned to the USS *Decatur*, DD-936, his third time at sea since joining the Navy. The *Decatur* took him on at least two deployments north of the Arctic Circle, down through the Mediterranean, then through the Suez Canal, into the Arabian Sea and the Indian Ocean.

During his three years on the *Decatur*, he would have returned home at least once or twice. I was too young to remember, but knowing my father, I can imagine him sitting his boys down with each departure to say goodbye. With that would have come clear direction regarding our behavior. "I am going to be away for a while, and I need you both to be strong and help your mother. I don't want to come back and find out that you have made her life miserable. Do you hear me?" Our own call to duty was just one of the many ways we were taught to deal with saying goodbye.

His time on the *Decatur* ended abruptly on May 6, 1964, when it collided at sea with a much larger aircraft carrier, the USS *Lake Champlain*, following refueling operations, 150 miles off the coast of Virginia. While the ship sustained extensive damage, unlike Uncle Herbert's collision at sea, there were no reported fatalities. I can't help but wonder if his thoughts went back to his brother that day. In all the times he told the story about the *Decatur*'s collision, I have never heard him make that connection once, but how could it not have been on his mind?

After the *Decatur*, when I was five, we moved to Naples, Italy, where I met Fonceno, an Italian boy my age. He knew little English, if any, but he somehow taught me how to speak Italian. We were great friends and I spent countless hours with him over the three years we lived in Naples. The day I said goodbye to him in 1967, when Dad was transferred back to the States, was probably the last time I spoke Italian with anyone.

From 1967 to 1971 we lived in Bainbridge, Maryland, where I met Jerry. He and his parents lived in the apartment downstairs. He was in the fourth grade, I was in the third, and we were in Mrs. McDowell's mixed classroom together. Jerry and I were best friends, as were our parents. Then there was Alan, who moved into Jerry's place when the Navy transferred Jerry's father. Paul lived across the hall from Alan. In 1971 my father was transferred to Virginia, where he would eventually retire, but not until we'd lived in three different places: Yorktown, Williamsburg, and Norfolk.

There are so many people who came into and then left my life as we moved from one place to another. In those days, when you moved there was no looking back. There was no email, Facebook, or Instagram. Even a phone call was long distance and that cost money. The list of friends I said goodbye to over my life is long. I am so envious of people who talk about how they still have close relationships with childhood friends. Not me. Other than a few I have connected with on Facebook, most are only a vague memory today. In my mind, I can hear Raúl Juliá's line in the 1976 movie *The Gumball Rally*, as he rips off the rearview mirror from the sports car he is sitting in. "The first rule of Italian driving is what's behind me is not important." Somewhere along the way I got good at saying goodbye, and I learned not to look back.

One of the more prominent figures from my childhood was my maternal grandfather, who, unlike Dad's father, I was very close to. Julius Hector Pachor was born in 1896 in Lussinpiccolo, a small Italian village on the northeastern coast of the Adriatic. Jules left Lussinpiccolo in 1914 at the young age of seventeen as a merchant marine on board a small, 6,744-gross ton, Austria-Hungry freighter, the SS *Lucia*. He arrived in Pensacola, Florida, in July of that year, and one year later, on August 8, 1915, he applied for US citizenship.

Jules had a lifelong love of the sea that stayed with him until he died. Over the years he had several sailboats including a large two-mast schooner that he had purchased for a bargain when some long-forgotten gangster was sent to prison. I have fond memories of him on his last sailboat, which he kept in Florida, where he spent his winters after retiring. I have memories of him sitting in the breezeway in his home in Connecticut, listening to the Italian opera on the radio. I remember him visiting us in Naples where, thanks to Fonceno, I was able to speak to my grandfather in his native tongue. I suspect that helped strengthen the bond between us.

I remember how excited I was that my grandfather was going to be visiting us just before Christmas one year, on his way to Florida for the winter. I was fourteen and had just started my freshman year at York High, in Yorktown. I was home alone on December 3, 1973, two days before he was to arrive, when the phone rang.

"Hi, honey. It's your Aunt Norma. Is your mom there?"

"No, they went out for dinner. They should be home soon, though."

"Okay. Please tell her to call me as soon as she gets home. Her father just died."

He had suffered a massive heart attack and died instantly as he was wiping down his car in preparation to leave the next morning to see us.

It's telling that I have such fond memories of my grandfather, but I have only a vague memory of the sadness at hearing the news of his death, and I have little more than a snapshot in my mind of his funeral. How could I have such little memory of a loss so significant in my life? I loved my grandfather and there is no doubt he loved me. His death would have undoubtedly been a huge loss to me, but as I look back on that time in my life it just seems to be one of the facts of my life. What's behind me is not important.

I had mastered the "first rule of Italian driving." I see it everywhere in my life to this day. Once someone or something is gone, I rarely if ever look back. My wife, Marilyn, and I are very different in that regard. Not only does she have a long list of friends whom she has known for decades, we have a house full of possessions that she hangs on to because of the memories they are connected to. For example, when we sold our last motorcycle, after my eyesight got too bad for us to ride safely, I immediately gave away my helmets and all my riding gear. That chapter was over, and I saw no reason to hang on to the remnants of it. Marilyn insisted on keeping her helmet even though she doesn't ride. We had far too many good times on the bike for her to just get rid of it. For her, the memories bring her comfort. For me, they are only a reminder of the loss, so I move on.

Turning my back on so many good friends and fond memories would have taken its toll on me. It would have been hard to feel the stability under my feet that it takes to help a young boy feel secure. By the time I was a teenager, fear had become an ever-present companion in my life. It takes little imagination today for me to see that the scared little boy that my therapist, Chad, and I had discussed wasn't just an abstract feeling. He was me.

Following the death of my grandfather, my parents began to feel that I was less focused on my schoolwork and started to worry about my future. When my father received orders transferring him to Tehran, Iran, later that year, they knew they had to do something. This was prior to the Iranian Revolution, and we had good diplomatic relationships with the Shah's government, but neither of my parents felt like it was the right environment for me or for my mother. Dad opted to take an unaccompanied tour of duty, which meant that while he would only be there for one year he would have to go alone, leaving his family behind. My brother had enlisted in the Navy by then and was no longer living at home, so it would have been just Mom and me. They decided that the best thing for me was to attend a boarding school, Frederick Military Academy, about forty-five minutes away in Portsmouth, Virginia.

In the fall of 1974, about the same time my dad left for Tehran, I packed my bags and checked into my new home at Frederick. I was only fifteen and for the first time in my life I wasn't living at home, at least not full-time. I did well academically and, more importantly, the experience helped me find an inner strength that I'd never realized I had. The person who helped me more than anyone to see that was my wrestling coach.

Up until then, unlike my brother, I had shown very little interest in sports. I had played Little League baseball for a while, but it was never my thing. I was more interested in picking daisies in the outfield than I was in the game. When we lost our catcher and the coach put me behind that plate, I hated it and was never any good. That was the end of my sports career until I got to Frederick.

I no longer recall if it was a requirement to participate in a sport at Frederick or if it was just that most of the boys I knew chose to do so. Whatever the motivation, I decided I would try out for basketball. I knew very little about the sport, but I figured that as one of the tallest kids in my class it was a natural choice. With a little coaching, I thought I could be good. I never made it past the first day of tryouts. In fact, the way I remember it, I ran a couple of layup drills before hearing, "You can go." I will never forget how embarrassed I was. Getting cut so early with so little empathy stung, and I vowed that I would not let that happen again. I was suddenly very motivated to find a sport that would make me strong and prove to everyone that I wasn't just some scared little boy.

I signed up for the wrestling team. I knew even less about wrestling, except that it was a sport of individual strength and speed. Man against man. I would not be able to hide in the outfield and pick daisies. Wrestling would make me strong, and it would make me a man—either that or I'd get killed in the process.

I looked ridiculous in the skimpy wrestling singlet we had to wear. There was no way to hide the fact that I was little more than skin and bones. Why the coach took a chance with me I will never know. I am not sure if he was having difficulty fielding a full team or if he just needed a practice dummy for the more seasoned wrestlers.

Seeing Clearly

The coach pushed me harder than I had ever been pushed in my life. There was more than one occasion when I was ready to quit but he just wouldn't let me. I would love to say that thanks to my coach I became a star wrestler, winning state championships, but that isn't how it went. In fact, I was never more than an average wrestler. For most of the time I was little more than a practice dummy for the better wrestlers, but it tested me physically and mentally. At first, I was terrified each time I got in the ring. With time, I started to realize that while I may not be a great wrestler, I could, if equally matched, hold my own. For the first two years, Coach Smith would occasionally put me in matches, but I lost more than I won.

In my senior year, the starting wrestler we had in the 181-pound weight class had graduated or changed schools and there was no one else to step into the starting lineup except me. At the time, I weighed just barely over 170. That meant I would be giving up ten pounds to most opponents.

As we approached the final match of the season, I had won almost half my matches. If I could win this last match, I would earn a letter! Unlike my brother, whom I am sure had lettered in multiple sports in high school, I had never achieved anything in sports. Winning that match was important to me, and the thought of losing was unbearable. It would only reinforce my forever-present sense of inadequacy.

In high school wrestling, as the season progresses, the maximum weight increases over the course of the season so by the last match, my opponents could be much closer to 190. I was still barely over 170, so by the end of the year I could be wrestling someone as much as twenty pounds heavier—a significant weight advantage for my opponent. Prior to each match, each wrestler had to weigh in to make sure they were below the maximum weight for their weight class. The weigh-in can be a dramatic event. It is the first time you see who you will be wrestling as you each step on the scale.

Our coach believed the match started with the mental game at the weigh-in. "Don't give them any sense that they may have a weight advantage over you. When you step on that scale, I don't care how far below weight you are, I want you to step on carefully. Act like you have no idea if you will make your weight." To drive the point home, he insisted that everyone strip down prior to being weighed. The wrestling uniform was humiliating enough for me as a tall, skinny kid. Naked, there was no way to hide that I was well below the upper limit of the weight class.

I did as I was instructed. As I waited to face my opponent for the first time, I took off my clothes and carefully stepped on the balanced beam scale. Good news—the needle didn't move. Of course not! Everyone in the room knew the outcome long before I stepped on. I could have jumped on it fully dressed wearing combat boots and there would have been little more than a wiggle on the needle.

After the official proclaimed that I qualified to wrestle, a guy stepped forward from the back of the group on the other team. He too was naked, but the outcome of his weigh-in was far more in question. He stepped on the scale slowly. Delicately. The needle on the scales lifted and wiggled a bit. At first, I didn't think he would make it. No one did. But then it hovered just below. As far as I could tell he didn't have an ounce to spare. I would be giving up every bit of twenty pounds today.

After the weigh-in, the coach and Sean, the wrestler in the weight class right above me—the unlimited weight class—pulled me aside. The coach started, "Chris, the guy you will be wrestling is their unlimited weight class wrestler. I am not sure how he qualified for 181 but he did. He is good. He beat Sean when they wrestled in the last match, but it was very close. I think they moved him down when they saw that he would have a big weight advantage over you. He needs this win to make it to the state championships."

Seeing Clearly

Shit! Sean was one of our best wrestlers on the team. We had wrestled countless times in practice, and it was never close with me. I was screwed. There would be no letter and I was about to get my ass kicked again.

The coach knew I was afraid. And he knew what was at stake for me. I don't think he was trying to scare me, but he needed me to know this was going to take my A-game.

"You can win this match, Chris," Coach said. "Sean can give you some tips from the last time they wrestled."

"Coach is right," Sean said. "You can win this, Chris. He is big and he is strong, but he is slow. You just need to keep moving. Don't ever let him get a hold of you and never let him get on top. If you do, you're dead."

By the time we got to the 181-pound weight class our team was losing. We needed to win the last two, mine and Sean's, if the team was to win the last match of our season.

As I got ready to walk on the mat the coach grabbed me by the shoulders, spun me around, looked me in the eyes, and said, "I can tell you are scared, Chris, but I need you to believe this: You can win this! Just get out there and do exactly what Sean said, and you will win. Do you believe me?"

"Yes," I lied.

As I walked out on the mat it felt like everyone watching, me included, knew how this was going to end. The tall, skinny kid was about to get his ass kicked. I could hear his teammates screaming and laughing. They could smell the victory.

There was a lot at stake for both of us. Our match could decide which team won that day. My opponent wanted to go to the state championships; I desperately wanted to not get killed. The thought of earning a letter was long gone. Survival was the only thought in my mind.

Chris, you have to focus. Don't be afraid. Listen to the coach. Just keep moving. You can do this, I tried to convince myself.

When the whistle blew, I did as I had been told: I moved as fast as I could.

I got lucky with a quick take-down. *Okay, just hold him. Don't try for anything more! Just stay on top for as long as you can.*

He was strong and I imagine it looked like some skinny kid riding a bull. I felt him fight for position, and just as he was about to grab my leg I immediately let go and jumped back.

Don't let him get a hold of you. Move. Move. Move!

Then I did it again: another take-down. As soon as I felt him find some stability I let go and jumped back. No way I was going to let him get a hand on me.

Then I did it again, and again.

I had no idea if I was scoring points—I was just staying alive. That's all I needed to do.

When the official raised my hand over my head as the winner at the end of that match my team went crazy. No one, especially me, had thought I had a chance. I will never forget the pride and satisfaction on the coach's face as I walked off the mat a winner. He was right. I could do it, and I did. Sean easily won the last match and our team left victorious that day. Before we left, the other coach came up to ours and asked, "Where did you get that guy at 181? We were sure we had that one."

I was still a tall, skinny kid who looked ridiculous in a wrestling singlet, far from an intimidating athlete, but I had a taste of what I could do if I just stopped being afraid and I wanted more. I was tired of feeling like a scared little boy. It was time to leave him behind and to pretend he never existed.

As graduation drew near, I started looking for colleges. Thanks to my parents' decision to send me to Frederick, I had good grades

Seeing Clearly

and solid SAT scores, so I had plenty of options, but I only remember applying to three schools: Old Dominion University near my home; the University of Maryland, my brother's alma mater; and the Virginia Military Institute in Lexington, Virginia. I have no idea if I was ever accepted by the first two because, almost from the first time I heard about it, I knew I would go to VMI.

I wasn't really looking for another military school experience. In fact, I am pretty sure it was just the opposite. After three years in a military high school and growing up in a Navy family I was far more interested in either following in my brother's footsteps at Maryland or ODU, where I could be near my friends. So, when a recent Frederick graduate, and VMI student, came back to speak to our senior class I really wasn't interested. He happened to be an electrical engineering student, the degree I was interested in pursuing, and as he talked about the well-respected engineering program there, he piqued my interest, but I still wasn't sold. As he talked about how demanding the school was, not just academically but mentally and physically, there was little doubt this was far more demanding than Frederick. Then he added, "Not everyone can make it there." That's when I knew I would go to VMI. My experience at Frederick Military Academy and the wrestling team had given me just enough confidence to want more.

The Virginia Military Institute is in the Shenandoah Valley in the small, historic town of Lexington, Virginia. By far, the most prominent structure on the post is the ominous four-story barracks, which serves as the dormitory for the Corps of Cadets. As you enter the barracks the words "You May Be Whatever You Resolve To Be" are boldly inscribed above you—not what you want to be, but what you "Resolve" to be. The distinction is immediately clear as you pass through the archway.

The barracks is unwelcoming and unforgiving. It is open in the center, with concrete walkways and steel railings around each of the four floors. It looks far more like a prison than a college dormitory. The words that sold me on VMI echoed in my mind: "Not everyone can make it there," and I thought, *Can I? Do I have the resolve?*

At the same time there was a feeling of pride, of belonging to something so much larger than I had ever been a part of. I was part of a heritage dating back to 1839. I think that as scared as I was that day, I was far more afraid of what it would mean if I failed. I had come so far from that scared little boy who was fearful of his own shadow. This is what I had asked for—something that would finally let me forever leave that weak little boy in my rearview mirror. That's when I knew, with absolute certainty, that there could only be one answer to my question about whether I could make it there. *I have to...somehow.* If I didn't, I would never be more than a fearful little kid.

The Corps of Cadets live on each of the floors in inverse order according to their relative importance. First classmen, or seniors, live on the ground floor; second classmen, or juniors, on the second; and third classmen on the third. The fourth floor is reserved for the newest members of the Corps of Cadets—"Rats" as they are known for much of their first year before they earn the right to even be called fourth classmen.

Shortly after saying goodbye to my parents, I was led politely to the basement of the barracks where everything changed in an instant. The first thing we learned was to "strain." Straining is a rigid posture that every Rat must maintain when in the barracks and outside of a room. Your fingers are curled into a fist and pressed tightly to your side, your shoulders are pinned back with your chest out and your chin pulled back tightly to your chest. Your eyes are locked straight forward and NEVER looking into the eyes of the person speaking to you.

One of the third classman jammed a small red book in my face and barked, "This is your Rat Bible. Read and memorize every

Seeing Clearly

word in there! God help you if you lose it!" Then I was instructed to turn and face the wall, straining and holding my Rat Bible in front of my face.

Someone made the mistake of turning their head to ask a follow-up question, but before the words left his mouth, he was nearly attacked by one of the uniformed upperclassmen there.

"Why the fuck are you looking at me? Do you think I am pretty? Do you want to fuck me?"

"Ahhh, no, I just…"

"Shut up and turn around and read your goddamn Rat Bible."

We stood that way while, one at a time, we were taken in to get our uniforms and to get our heads shaved.

The Rat Bible was filled with the history of the school and the surrounding area, local scenic attractions such as the Natural Bridge as well as the rules and regulations that all Keydets must follow, and countless random facts such as the weight and muzzle velocity of our standard-issue M14 rifle. All facts that you were expected to recite, verbatim, at a moment's notice.

When in the barracks, not only are all Rats required to be constantly straining, but they must also follow a very specific path down each walkway and up all three flights of stairs to get to their rooms, and they must do so in single file. The simple act of returning to your room could be an ordeal. Anywhere along that path any upperclassman could stop you for literally any reason and, if the Rat in front was stopped, everyone behind him stopped. Sometimes it was simply a first classman trying to figure out if it was worth heading to the mess hall for breakfast that morning.

"Hey, Menu! What's for breakfast?"

"Sir, this morning the Corps will be dining on fried eggs, grits, bacon, and orange juice," the Rat would answer hopefully. If not, you could be there a while.

If you ran into someone who was feeling playful, he might stop you with, "Whoa, Rat! What's the Natural Bridge worth?"

To which the proper response was the exact wording in your Rat Bible. "Sir, the Natural Bridge is well worth a visit by every cadet and their family."

If you ran into someone who was feeling particularly ornery, the quiz could be more challenging, such as, "What's the inscription on the parapet, Rat?"

I have no idea how many times I stood there straining behind a line of brother Rats while the one in the front stumbled through the correct answer: "The healthful and pleasant abode of a crowd of honorable youths, pressing up the hill of science with noble emulation. A gratifying spectacle. An honor to our country and our state. Objects of honest pride to their instructors and fair specimens of citizen soldiers attached to their native state. Proud of her fame and ready in every time of deepest peril to vindicate her honor and defend her rights."

The list of things a Rat was expected to memorize seemed endless. Failing an impromptu quiz from an upperclassman as you made your way to your room could result in a public berating at minimum, or at worse a visit to the Rat Disciplinary Committee for a personal "sweat party," a one-on-one workout with a seriously aggravated upperclassman.

Even if your memory was perfect, it didn't mean you would get away without a sweat party. Randomly, an hour or so before the bugler sounded reveille, signaling it was time to wake up, someone would kick down your door and you would be on your face doing pushups before you even knew what was going on.

All that with a full academic load, five and a half days of classes, the weekly Saturday Noon Inspection of your room, and the demanding course work required for the electrical engineering degree I was pursuing. Without question, this was a lot harder than Frederick.

Seeing Clearly

During those early days, there were times when I felt overwhelmed and I was afraid I might break down and cry, but as a Rat you learn quickly not to show such weakness and vulnerability—something I was prepared for thanks to my father. I saw brother Rats, on more than one occasion, break down in tears in front of an upperclassman—and that is like throwing gas on a fire. Any sign of weakness was rewarded with screams of laughter and insults. If my wrestling experience had given me some sense of my ability to push aside fear, my Rat year at VMI was an advanced degree in swallowing pain.

By any measure, physical, mental, or emotional, the Virginia Military Institute was one of the most demanding experiences of my life. It was also one of the most rewarding. I would like to say that when I graduated four years later, my insecurities were a thing of the past, but that would be a lie. I had, however, become pretty good at hiding them, even from myself.

I was a graduate of one of the toughest schools I could attend, and I was an officer in the United States Marine Corps. The way I saw it, they both gave me a level of credibility and the perception of someone far more confident than I really felt. I did everything I could to live up to that. I had done everything I could to get rid of the scared little boy, to leave him behind just like he had done to so many others, but in my quietest moments I still felt his presence. It wouldn't be long before he would start to act out, setting my life on a far more circuitous course than I had ever imagined.

7

Mutual Assured Destruction

OVER THE LAST FEW YEARS, I have spent a lot of time looking back on my life, trying to make meaning from some of the more memorable events. If it wasn't for the relentless progression of retinal disease, robbing me of the faces of the people I love the most, I may never have seen some of the examples of how I spent so much of my life acting blindly. There were some huge mistakes that I made in my forties, but as I look back I can see the presence of warning signs even in my early twenties.

During the summer break between my freshman and sophomore years at VMI, I drove to Statesville, North Carolina, to visit one of my roommates, Doug. One of his sisters, Mary Hatley, was seventeen. I think I may have spent more time with her during that visit than I did with Doug. By the time I went back to my home in Norfolk, Virginia, I was in love. I'd had a few other girlfriends over the years, but Hatley was, without question, my first real love.

She was two years younger than me, so she still had one year of high school left, and when she graduated, she went to college at Randolph-Macon Woman's College in Lynchburg, Virginia, only forty-five minutes away from VMI. With her that close we got to see

Seeing Clearly

each other a lot more and our relationship grew stronger. She was all I could think of and there was no doubt in my mind, or probably in anyone's who knew us, that we had a good chance of being together forever. At the time, I couldn't imagine any other future.

Then one day in the middle of my senior year, I called her to tell her I wanted to break up. It wasn't planned. There wasn't a fight. There wasn't another girl. I am certain I was still in love, but I just ended it. When she asked why, I think I said something like, "I just think it's time." I can't imagine what that must have been like for her.

Today, forty years later, I have some idea of the reason. Graduation was approaching and immediately following that I would be commissioned as a second lieutenant in the Marine Corps. With that would come orders to The Basic School, TBS, in Quantico, Virginia, and before the end of the year I would be off to somewhere else. I knew the drill from watching my father's career in the Navy. The next several years of my life were no longer in my control. Hatley still had two years of college to complete, and she was planning to spend the next year studying abroad. She rightfully wasn't willing to give up her education to follow me, and I had no option about joining the Corps. We were going to be apart for the next two years. I would guess that I saw our relationship was coming to an end and decided to be proactive. What's behind me is not important…only this time she wasn't behind me quite yet.

My class graduated on May 27, 1981, but thanks to one of the dumber moves in my life my diploma reads September of that year unlike the rest of my brother Rats. I was taking a political science course that last semester and as the end of the year approached, I had a solid grade. I did the math and realized that even if I got a zero on the final paper that was due on the last day of class, I would still get a C. The way I saw it, the paper would make no difference in my future, and I decided not to do it. I was so wrong. The one variable I didn't factor into my math equation was a grade of "Incomplete."

The professor was clear: he would be more than happy to accept my paper late, but he would not do so until at least one week after graduation.

My family was already in Lexington when I got the news that I would not graduate with my class. I will never forget driving over to their hotel to tell them they could go home. It was one of the most embarrassing moments of my life. The paper was, fittingly, on the nuclear doctrine of Mutual Assured Destruction, and when I turned it in two weeks later, I got an A. It also delayed my commissioning as a second lieutenant in the Marine Corps. As a result, I would start Basic School six weeks later rather than with the other Marine officers from my class. The six-week delay in starting TBS may have had even bigger implications than I realized at the time.

Hatley came up with her parents to Lexington at the end of the school year to pick up her brother. It had been six months since we broke up. The instant I saw her I realized what a mistake I had made. I was still hopelessly in love. I couldn't just walk away, and I asked her if there was any way she could forgive me and give it one more chance.

She looked at me for a few moments, processing what she had just heard. There was little expression on her face to give me a hint of what she was thinking. Then she said, almost matter-of-factly, "Kiss me."

I did, and if there had been any doubts in my mind they were gone, but her face still showed little expression.

"Why did you ask me to do that, Hatley?"

"I just needed to know that there was still something there."

"And?" I asked.

"Yes," she said as a big smile came across her face.

To this day my heart still melts just remembering her smile. I loved her so much.

Seeing Clearly

Then Hatley, Doug, and the rest of their family loaded up the car and headed home to North Carolina. Later that summer, as planned, I reported for training at the Marine Corps Training Center in Quantico, Virginia, six hours by car from Statesville.

Our long-distance relationship would not survive the summer.

I had not been at Quantico long when Hatley drove up from Statesville for a long weekend. One of my roommates at Quantico, coincidentally named Doug, was casually dating another Marine officer, Kathleen, who was six weeks behind us in training and we made plans for the four of us to have dinner together that weekend. I wasn't a huge fan of Kathleen, but Doug and I had become good friends.

All night long Kathleen and I took potshots at each other. We were never actually arguing, but there was no mistaking that we didn't like each other. At the end of the evening Doug and Kathleen headed in one direction, Hatley and I in another.

"Good night, Doug," I said.

"Good night, Chris. See you in the morning," replied Doug.

"Good night, Kathleen."

Nothing.

As the distance grew between us, I yelled, "GOOD NIGHT, KATHLEEN!"

"Do the letters F O mean anything to you, Chris?" was her response.

Hatley probably had enough of the bickering and said, "Oh come on, Chris. Just leave her alone. She is in a foul mood for some reason. Let's just go back to the hotel."

Only a few weeks later, I was having a conversation with our company commander when he asked, "What are you up to this weekend, Monnette?"

"I am driving down to North Carolina, sir. I have to break up with my girlfriend."

"North Carolina! Isn't that a six-hour drive?"

"Yes, sir."

"Do you want to borrow a dime for the payphone?" he asked with a laugh.

"No, sir. I already did that to her once. I need to do this one in person."

Unlike when we broke up in my senior year, this time I had an explanation, although I still didn't know the real reason. Somewhere in the weeks following Hatley's visit, Doug and Kathleen had stopped dating and Kathleen and I had decided to pursue a relationship. I am not sure why I didn't see the red flags at the time. My relationship with Kathleen was tumultuous from the day I met her, and it never changed. I remember Doug saying after observing an argument between Kathleen and me, "I am glad she's yours!"

"I am not sure why, Doug, but so am I" was all I could say.

Whatever the reason, this time, Hatley was unquestionably in my rearview mirror. My relationship with Kathleen assured that.

The night of my graduation from TBS, just before I headed west to Camp Pendleton, in Southern California, a small group of us, including Doug and Kathleen, got together to celebrate. I have a vague memory from that night of me loudly demanding that she marry me. It's possible that I was standing on the table at the time.

The marriage proposal makes a little more sense to me now. I was leaving for California the next day, 2,700 miles away. This was just like all those times my family had moved when I was growing up. We packed up everything we had and drove off, never looking back. This time I was a Marine officer, and it just wasn't okay to be afraid to be alone. I had become good at hiding my insecurities so it wasn't something I would have discussed with anyone, or even acknowledged to myself. With my blood alcohol content where it was that night, surrounded by friends whom I had lived and trained with for the last few months, I likely felt a moment of weakness. In that moment, that scared little child, whom I had worked so hard to ignore, suddenly spoke up. He didn't want to be alone, and he proposed to the one person he could hold on to at the time.

I cannot help but wonder how things would have been different had I turned in that paper on Mutual Assured Destruction on time. I would have started TBS six weeks earlier and I likely would have never met Kathleen. It's unlikely the relationship with Hatley would have survived much longer, but I almost certainly would not have been proposing to Kathleen that day.

The next morning Kathleen asked, "Do you remember what you asked me last night?"

"Ah, I think so. I think I asked you to marry me."

"You did. Did you mean it?"

While I have very vague memories of asking Kathleen to marry me that night, my response that morning is clearer.

"I guess so. Sure. Yeah. Let's do that," and we were engaged.

I wasn't in love. I wasn't thinking I wanted to spend my life with her. I was literally thinking, *Why not?*

I never asked Kathleen what she was thinking at the time. Why would she want to marry me at such a young age? Clearly, she knew as well as I did that our relationship was far from perfect. I guess we both had our reasons.

Following her graduation from TBS, six weeks after mine, she accepted an assignment in California so we could be together. We rented a tiny two-bedroom place in San Clemente that was walking distance from the beach.

We were married on September 4, 1982, in Kathleen's hometown of Columbus, Ohio, less than a year after the double date Hatley and I had with Doug and Kathleen. I have vague memories of our wedding. Much of it has been obscured by time, way too much liquor at the reception, and the "first rule of Italian driving."

There were over three hundred people in the church that day, mostly Kathleen's family and their friends. There may have been ten on the groom's side of the church: my parents, my brother, and his wife, Marilyn, a few of my friends from high school, and that's it. It never occurred to me, until recently, why my parents didn't invite other relatives. Sadly, thanks to our transient lifestyle, they just were not a big part of my life growing up. Mike and three of my closest friends were in my wedding party, but I am uncertain which of my friends was my best man. I would need to look at the photos again to be sure, but I got rid of those years ago. They were no longer relevant.

My memories from that day are all vague, with one exception. I remember with absolute clarity standing at the front of the church. It was packed. There was the small contingent of my family on one side. The rest of the church was filled with faces I had never seen, most of whom I never saw again. As Kathleen began to walk down the aisle with her father by her side, I could see them both smiling. They were so happy. I can see Kathleen's gown—it was beautiful. I remember so clearly what was going through my mind at the time. *What the hell am I doing? Am I fucking crazy? I am not sure I even like her.* I looked around the church at the hundreds of faces. *It's probably just nerves. I bet everyone feels this way on their wedding day. Besides, it's too late now.*

While our marriage was rocky right from the start, we did have some great experiences. We explored Southern California for the first time together, and then the Corps sent us to Okinawa, Japan, and we got to experience that as well. Through it all there were a lot of laughs and plenty of good times, but when we fought, it was ugly. She would scream insults at me. I would respond with words carefully chosen to hurt as much as possible. When she got particularly mad, she would hit me.

Seeing Clearly

I remember one such argument, early in our relationship, when we were living in our tiny triplex in San Clemente. I couldn't tell you what we were arguing about, but we were both furious and the screams were flying. She suddenly punched me in the shoulder.

"Ow, that hurt! Kathleen, I have never hit a woman, but I swear to God if you hit me one more time…"

Wham! Another punch to the shoulder. I saw white. By the grace of God all I did was storm out the door.

Then I heard her slam the door, hard, behind me. *That's it. I've had it.* I turned around and headed back into the apartment, but she had locked the door and I didn't have my keys.

"Kathleen, open the door."

"NO!"

"Kathleen, open this goddamn door right now!"

"FUCK YOU!"

"I swear to God, I am going to count to three and then I am going to kick this door down."

"Go to hell."

"One. I am not kidding, Kathleen."

"You wouldn't dare!"

"Two. Kathleen?"

Not a sound from inside.

"Three!"

I wasn't a huge guy, but I was two hundred pounds and a reasonably fit Marine officer. When I threw myself at the door, it came from my toes. Unfortunately, half a second before my shoulder made contact, Kathleen turned the doorknob to open the door. It hit her hard and she flew across the room. My first thought as I saw her hit the ground was, *Oh my God, I have seriously hurt her. What have I done!*

Then I saw her stand up, uninjured, and I knew I had a problem. Hell hath no fury like a pissed off Woman Marine. I ran out the door, closing it solidly behind me.

Kathleen and I brought out the worst in each other and we were too young to figure out how to do anything different. But I never once considered divorce. I just didn't consider it an option. The one thing I knew growing up was that when you got married, it was for life. I could not even imagine telling my parents that I was considering a divorce. What a tremendous failure that would have been. I could almost hear my father's voice in my head: "I don't know, Julie. Why can't he be like his brother? That kid just has no commitment. When things get tough, he runs away."

That is not at all what he would have said, but I had created a set of expectations that would have been hard for anyone to live up to. Failing in something as important as a marriage wasn't something I could accept. If there was one thing I learned from my experiences at VMI and in the Corps, it was that I could do hard things. I could find a way to make the marriage with Kathleen work. There was potentially another factor at play as well. If we split up, I would be alone and that might have frightened me more than Kathleen ever could.

I got out of the Corps on April 1, 1985, and took a job as an electrical engineer at Hughes Aircraft Company. A little more than a year later Kathleen was transferred to Washington, DC, and we ended up living in Northern Virginia, close to where my brother would eventually move. With each passing year our relationship became more and more rocky. We seemed to fight constantly. In 1989 Kathleen was transferred again. This time to Panama. Like my father's assignment to Tehran, it was an unaccompanied assignment and I stayed in our home in Arlington. At the time, tensions between the United States and the dictator, Manuel Noriega, were reaching a peak. I don't recall the exact date, but I can remember the discussion clearly. I was sitting on the couch in our basement watching *Cheers* when the phone rang.

Seeing Clearly

"Hello."

It was my wife. "Chris, it's me!"

"Oh hey! What a surprise. How's it goin' down there? Sounds scary on the news."

"Man, it is getting crazy," she said. "I had a close call today."

"What happened?"

As she began to tell me her story, I can remember looking up at the TV. *Cheers* was one of my all-time favorite TV shows and Kathleen's call was right in the middle of a great episode—and there was no way to pause a live TV show in the '80s.

Kathleen explained how she had been driving a military jeep when she was stopped by armed Panamanian soldiers at a checkpoint. "They started questioning me and then suddenly one of the men grabbed me and tried to drag me out of the jeep! Fortunately, I was able to jerk free from him long enough to throw it in gear and stomp on the gas before he could grab me again."

"Wow. That must have been scary. Glad you are okay."

In the background I heard Norm say something on my TV followed by loud laughter. *Shit, I am going to miss this entire show!*

"Hell yeah! I was scared as shit," Kathleen said. "I thought for sure they were going to kidnap me or rape me!"

"Well, I am glad you are okay."

"You are 'glad I am okay'? Chris, what the fuck is going on? Am I boring you?"

That's when it suddenly hit me. I was listening to my wife tell me about an incredibly harrowing experience she had in a foreign country, basically a war zone, and I was more interested in a stupid TV show. *What am I doing?* With that thought came the sudden clarity that our marriage was over. It had been for years, but neither of us wanted to admit it.

"I...I don't know Kathleen. It's just. I am sorry. I know that was incredibly scary. I just. I mean. It just isn't working for us, Kathleen.

Come on. You have to see it too, don't you?"

That is how I told her our marriage was over. It wouldn't be the worst way I would end a relationship in my life, but it was far from the best.

While the decision to split up was suddenly crystal clear, the thought of how I would tell my parents about my failure wasn't. I knew how disappointed they would be in me, and I dreaded the look I would see in my father's eyes. My mother would be supportive and loving. She would never let on, but I knew that deep inside she would be disappointed, too.

I knew I couldn't simply call them with the news. They lived about four hours south of me in Virginia Beach and I needed to drive down and tell them face to face. I called my brother, who also lived in Northern Virginia, near me, to give him the news and get his advice.

"Oh, I am so sorry, Chris. You okay?"

"Yeah. It was time, Mike. It hasn't been good for a long time. I am just not sure how the hell I am going to tell Mom and Dad."

"What do you mean? They love you. You know they will be supportive."

"I don't know, Mike. I am just worried about how they will take the news."

"Tell you what, are you okay if I come down with you this weekend?"

"Man, you don't have to do that! I'll be okay."

"Hey, look, I haven't seen them in a while so I would love to go. And besides, I think you will see. It won't be as hard as you think."

When Mom first heard the news her immediate concerns were for me. "Oh, I am sorry, dear. Are you okay?"

"Yeah, Mom, I'm all right. It was time. I'm just sorry. I know this is probably a huge shock to you and Dad."

"Not really. We both could see how wrong the two of you were for each other. In fact, we kept praying that you would wake up at some point and realize that yourself."

"Are you kidding me? When did that start?"

"Oh my gosh, dear, right from the beginning. On the day you two got married, I was so upset."

"Mom, I wish you would have said something."

"Your father and I talked about how we wished we could talk you out of it, but we knew you wouldn't have listened, and you would have hated us if we tried! Would you have listened?"

"I honestly don't know, Mom, but I would love to have known that."

"I remember saying to your father, 'I wish I had Mary Hatley's number. She is the only one who could talk him out of this.'" There was more than a little truth to that statement.

For many years, I blamed that failed marriage on Kathleen, as if it were all her fault, but that was both unfair and inaccurate. The reality is that our biggest mistake was the flawed reasoning that brought us together in the first place. We should have never been married, but we were both looking to fill some hole in our lives and blindly entered a doomed relationship.

It is sad that I never told my parents how unhappy I was and that I was staying married largely because I was afraid that they would be disappointed in me. It is equally sad that they didn't tell me how much they had hoped I would see how wrong things were and move on because they didn't want to hurt me. It's amazing how one very authentic conversation between my parents and me might have changed things.

Kathleen's commanding officer allowed her to fly home to try and salvage our marriage. We used the time to find a cheap attorney to do the paperwork for us. I took my car, motorcycle, and half the furniture and found a small apartment nearby in Annandale. Our divorce was final six months later, on August 6, 1990, twenty-nine days shy of eight years. I guess we "gave it the old college try." I walked away and, as always, never looked back.

A year or so after Kathleen and I split up, I reached out to my old college roommate, Doug. That is when I learned that Mary Hatley had been living only fifteen minutes away from me for the last several years. She was living with her fiancé, and they were about to be married the next month. How ironic that I'd broken up with her because I was afraid of us being apart, and that for the last several years we had been almost neighbors.

Hatley and I met for dinner and caught up on all that had happened in our lives in the years since we had seen each other. As I sat across the table and looked at her, I knew just what a mistake I had made—twice. She asked me again, as she had that day we had broken up for the last time, "Why did you break up with me?"

"I don't know, Hatley. I really don't." It is only now that I have a sense of the answer to that question.

After dinner I walked her to her car, and she reached over and put her arm around me and leaned her head against my shoulder. We walked quietly, just remembering. We said goodbye and I never saw her again.

I have no misconception that Hatley and I were destined to be together forever. We were just kids, far too young to have any realistic expectation of such a future, but I find what happened between us so illustrative of my lack of emotional awareness at the time, and that would change little over the next twenty years.

I regret how I hurt Hatley, but even more so, I regret that the lessons I learned from the events of those years did not come until recently, far too late to prevent a personal disaster that would unravel my life and the lives of the people I loved most. That chapter was just beginning, and like what came before it, there were plenty of warning signs that I simply ignored.

8

A Glimpse Of Happiness

A PSYCHOLOGIST FRIEND OF MINE used to say, "If you had a parent or teacher in your life then you are screwed up." His point was, when we are born we are like a blank canvas, and from a very early age, our image of right and wrong is painted on us by the role models in our life. Much of those lessons come from modeling rather than being explicitly communicated, they are just "in-the-water." My role models were all very strong personalities, particularly my father, but it didn't stop there. Seven years in military schools and another four in the Marine Corps only ensured that before I was thirty the die was cast for me on how I viewed what was acceptable emotional behavior. Expressing anger was somehow appropriate, but being openly fearful just wasn't something that a man should ever do. I think I was in my late forties before I ever heard anyone suggest that vulnerability was anything except a bad idea for a man.

I can't say that my programming was all bad. I learned that I could handle far more pain and adversity than I had ever imagined as a scared young boy clinging to my mother for safety. That has frequently served me well, particularly in my career. I learned to take chances when, deep down, I was terrified that I might fail, but once you step off the ledge you only have one choice: You have to learn to fly, or your fate is clear. I have stepped off several in my career, which have paid off.

One of the most notable examples was my decision to change careers in 1987. I was complaining to my brother one day about how unchallenged I felt in the engineering job I had at the time, when he suggested that I consider a career change to sales. He had a successful sales career and thought that I could do the same. I was hesitant. I had more than my own fair share of insecurities and worried about my ability to be successful in sales. Mike was convinced it was the right move for me and really pushed me. When I first mentioned the idea to Kathleen, her response was, "Are you crazy? You don't know anything about sales. You'll never be successful. How will we pay the bills?" That gave me the motivation I needed to make the change. What I lacked in confidence, I more than made up in obstinance. The surest way to get me to do something is to tell me I am incapable of doing it. It's how I ended up at VMI.

I accepted a job as a sales rep with a regional distributor of computer graphics peripherals. It was a small company with a limited market, and it was a wonderful place to start out. I made $27,500 in my last full year as an engineer. By the time Kathleen and I split up less than three years later, my income had doubled, and more importantly, there was a seed of confidence that had begun to sprout inside me. Both would continue to grow over the next fifteen years until I stepped off one ledge too many and everything fell apart.

By the summer of 1990 I felt like my career was going in the right direction, but I saw the divorce as a big setback in my personal life. I remember feeling somewhat lonely, which today seems predictable given how few people I kept close to for most of my life. I seemed to crave connection with people, yet I was afraid of intimacy. I would guess I saw that as a risk, a ledge that was just too high to step off. It was far less risky to not let anyone in than it was to take a chance and lose someone I had opened my heart to.

Then, in late August 1990, the receptionist at work came into my office and said, "Hey, I know you are single now. Do you want to meet a friend of mine?"

Kathy was nineteen and frequently came into the office on Monday mornings with stories of wild parties and at least one Polaroid of a topless friend. I couldn't imagine any long-term relationship with one of her friends, but as she said, I was single.

"Sure. That would be great," I said.

"Great. Her name is Holly. She used to be my boss and I think the two of you would get along well. She is nice and she is pretty cute too!"

Her boss. Not the girl in the Polaroid? Well, that was probably more appropriate.

"Thanks, Kathy. She sounds wonderful. I would love to meet her."

"I hoped you would say that! Here's her business card. I already told her you would call," she said with a smile.

I pinned Holly's business card to my bulletin board in front of my desk and promised to call her that day.

When Holly and I spoke, I could tell right from the start that she was out of my league. She had a tremendous sense of confidence, she was outgoing, and when she told me where she lived, it was clear that she had been far more successful than me. Holly owned a condo, actually two, in Old Town Alexandria, one of the more desirable areas in Northern Virginia. Old Town was a historic district just across the river from Washington, DC, with cobblestone streets and eighteenth century townhomes. There were dozens of bars and fabulous restaurants within walking distance from Holly's condo. I rented an apartment fifteen minutes away in a nondescript high-rise building in Annandale, lost in a sea of strip malls and apartment buildings. I could barely afford to eat in Old Town let alone live there. We seemed to live worlds apart and I was intimidated before I even met her. We made plans to meet that night for dinner.

That afternoon, I was meeting with a customer in my office when suddenly he stopped in the middle of our conversation and asked, "How do you know Holly?"

"Who?" I asked.

He pointed to the business card on my bulletin board. "Her!"

"Oh! Her. Well, I don't actually know her, at least not really. I've never met her. Kathy, our receptionist, used to work for her and, well, she set us up. I have a date with her tonight."

"Oh."

"Wait! Do you know her?" I asked.

"Yeah. She's a bitch."

It's interesting to me now to think about that comment. Over my career, I have had more than one person share similar feedback about how they experienced me when we first met. In my case, instead of saying I was a "bitch," they would say that I was "intimidating" or "uncaring," which doesn't feel like who I have ever been, but given how guarded I can be with my emotions I can see how they may have felt that way about me. As I would soon learn, Holly and I were far more alike than I realized in that regard.

I am no longer certain what I was expecting that evening. I am sure that had I been asked, I would have never said that I was meeting my future wife. I think I just hoped she wasn't really a bitch. For our date, I put on the best suit I owned; I didn't get the sense that Holly was a casual type of woman.

The first thing I realized when Holly opened the door was that Kathy hadn't been completely forthcoming when she said that Holly was "pretty cute." She was beautiful. She was tall, elegantly dressed, with a great figure, and beautiful eyes. I liked her immediately. The confidence and charm that I'd heard on the phone were even more evident in person, and I could tell that she saw something in me that she liked as well.

After a glass of wine at her place, we walked to a nearby Italian restaurant for dinner where she gave me a small clue about her personality. As the waiter was discussing the specials that evening, he leaned forward as if to let us in on a secret and said, "I wouldn't recommend that one if you will be kissing later."

"I'll have that," Holly shot back so quickly that the waiter's words still seemed to linger in the air as she spoke. She looked at me and smiled at her joke, but somehow, I could tell she was also making it clear how things were going to go that evening. Holly liked to be in charge, and that was evident right from the beginning.

Not to be outdone, I said to the waiter, "I'll have the same thing." Then I looked at Holly, smiled, and said, "I really like garlic."

I was hooked on Holly from the start. She was everything that I wanted to be—successful, confident, outgoing—and on top of that there was a strong physical attraction. We started seeing each other regularly. After a few months I was beginning to feel that our relationship had grown into something more than just casual dating—certainly, it had for me, but I wasn't completely sure how Holly felt. It was always difficult for me to get a sense of what was in Holly's heart, and back then, when our relationship was brand new, I had no idea. She seemed interested, but at the same time she kept me at arm's distance.

So, one day, while sitting in a pizzeria in Old Town, I asked her, "Holly, are you seeing anyone else?" I remember feeling very nervous and vulnerable and had carefully rehearsed the question in my mind before asking it. I was prepared for her to say, "Yes," "No," or even "None of your business," but just as fast as she had told the waiter on our first date that she would be having the garlic dish, Holly snapped back with, "Always assume I am."

I was confused and more than a little embarrassed by my show of vulnerability. I had no idea what she was trying to tell me. Rather than ask for clarification I simply responded with, "Okay," and we finished our pizza. By the time I got home that night, my embarrassment had morphed into hurt and anger, and for a few days following that conversation, I thought seriously about abandoning any hopes of a relationship with Holly and just walking away without so much as a phone call. Given my history, I am surprised that I didn't do that, but by then, it was already too late for me to just walk away.

If there were other men, I would just have to win her over. It seems unthinkable to me today that we just let that sit there and moved on, as if nothing had been said. Many years later I asked her what she meant by that comment and I am still not sure I can explain what she was trying to tell me that day in the pizzeria. That was the way our relationship would go for the next seventeen years. There was frequently a lot left unsaid, or at least unheard, by both of us.

By the spring of 1991, as the lease on my apartment was about to expire, I had been spending most of my time at Holly's. We decided that I would give up my apartment and move in with her. No need to pay for two places. That created a new problem: She had no plans to give up any of her furniture to make room for mine. There was room for me, my stereo, my clothes, and little else.

As the last few days of my lease approached, I had done little to figure out a plan for my stuff beyond putting an ad on the apartment building bulletin board. I don't know if I was subconsciously dragging my feet because I was afraid to give up my furniture or if I was just being lazy. Whatever the reason, as the last weekend before I had to be out of my apartment approached, I still had no plan for my furniture. I had a large countertop microwave, some bedroom furniture, a small dining room set, and a large sectional in the living room.

Seeing Clearly

On the Saturday night before I had to be out, I was in a bit of a panic. I was sitting alone in my apartment looking around at all the stuff I had to get rid of in less than twenty-four hours. I would have to find a storage place, rent a U-Haul, and then convince a friend to give up their Sunday, at the last minute. It was an impossible task, and I was completely overwhelmed. As I sat there trying to figure out what to do first, my phone rang.

"Hi. I saw on the bulletin board downstairs that you have a microwave for sale. Is it still available?"

"Yes, it is! You live in the building? Do you want to come up and check it out?"

"Can I? That would be great. I will be right there."

She was about my age and there was a sadness in her eyes that suggested some challenging times. She saw the microwave and we agreed on $50 and I offered to carry it to her apartment for her. As we were about to leave, she looked in the living room. "Oh is that the sectional you are selling?"

"Yes, it is." I think I was asking $1,000. Kathleen and I had paid a lot more.

"Wow! I really like that. I wish we could afford that," she said, and we walked out the door with the microwave in hand.

Her place was stark, almost empty, and her husband was laying on the couch, clearly ill. Not the flu—this was something worse. I dropped off the microwave in the kitchen, collected my $50, and headed toward the door and then stopped and looked back at her and her husband.

"Do you want that sectional?"

"I would love it, but we can't afford it."

"Tell you what, if you help me carry it down it's yours."

Before the night was over, we had carried down not only the sectional but every other stick of furniture in the house. I kept the $50 for the microwave.

The furniture did not mean much to me. It was little more than a memory of a failed marriage, and it was probably somewhat cathartic to let it go. It was also consistent with how I had learned to handle change in my life—what's behind me is not important. As I loaded the car with my last few possessions and headed toward Old Town, I suddenly realized what I had done. I had burned the bridge behind me. If my relationship with Holly didn't work out, I had little more than my clothes to fall back on, but that was a brief thought; I was in love and I could not imagine any other outcome but spending the rest of our lives together.

Holly and I were married on the second anniversary of our first date, August 29, 1992. It was a small wedding, nothing like the big ceremony in Columbus with hundreds of people I had never seen before. We were married in the historic Christ Church in Old Town Alexandria, where Robert E. Lee and his family had worshiped nearly two hundred years before. We had about eighty people at our reception; I think fewer than twenty attended the actual wedding. This time there were no second thoughts, no fears, and my parents were equally thrilled. I remember feeling very emotional as we recited our vows. Holly held my hands and looked into my eyes with an encouraging smile as if to say, "You can do it." She of course had no issue with hers. She was always better at controlling her emotions than me.

Things happened quickly for us over the next few years. Only a few months after our wedding, my company was acquired by a much larger company, and we were relocated to Atlanta. Then, less than a year after we got to Atlanta, in early 1994, we got more great news when we learned that Holly was pregnant. She was due at the end of September. Soon we would be a family! Whatever mistakes I had made in my first marriage, they were long behind me now.

Seeing Clearly

Everything just seemed to be working out perfectly for us.

Then came the next big surprise. Not long after we learned that she was pregnant, I was promoted to regional sales manager for the Central US, the first of several promotions I would get over the next decade with my new company. The only bad news was we would need to move again, this time to Cincinnati. With a baby on the way, Cincinnati worked out great for us. It was only a hundred miles north of where Holly's parents lived, and it had a great airport. I would be traveling a lot with this job, and having her family within driving distance was a huge help.

With her due date at the end of September, I suggested we move in the spring so we could be settled before the baby arrived. Holly had found a great-paying job in Atlanta and did not want to give it up until she had to. She insisted on waiting until early September, only a few weeks before her due date. I wasn't thrilled about the idea of moving so late in her pregnancy, but she wouldn't budge, and when she made up her mind there was little chance of changing it.

On August 23, about a week shy of our two-year anniversary, I was in my hotel room somewhere near Dallas, getting ready for the day's sales calls with a couple of colleagues, when my cell phone rang. It was Holly.

"I stopped by the post office on the way to work this morning and while I was waiting in line, I think my water broke."

"What! You're kidding, right?" I felt a wave of panic wash over me. She wasn't due for nearly six weeks! I sank back on to the edge of the bed, staring at the floor.

I knew it. I knew it. Why the hell did she have to insist on waiting until the last minute to move?

"Don't worry. I think everything is fine. It didn't seem like a lot of fluid."

I was certain that the growing panic deep in my gut was going to consume me, but Holly didn't sound afraid or even nervous at all. She sounded irritated. In fact, she was furious.

"I just can't believe that asshole at the post office. I asked the manager if I could use their bathroom and he refused. 'Sorry, employees only.' I pleaded with him. He could see that I'm pregnant! Finally, I just yelled at him, loud enough for the whole place to hear, 'Look, I am pregnant, and I think my water just broke. I NEED to use your bathroom now!' He finally agreed and let me in."

I couldn't believe it. She was more upset about the manager at the post office than her water breaking. Didn't she see that this was a big deal? How could she not be at least a little scared? It made no sense to me. Maybe I was the one who was over-reacting?

"What are you going to do now?" I asked.

"I came home to take a shower. I already have a doctor's appointment scheduled today so I will just see what he says then. Don't worry. I am sure everything is fine."

"I can't stay here, Holly. I am going to catch the next flight back."

"No, don't. Really. I am sure it's okay. I will call you after I see him."

"Are you sure? Holly, this seems like a big deal to me."

"I am fine! Don't do anything yet. I will let you know what the doctor says. I promise."

"Okay. I'll wait until you talk to him, but call him, please?"

"I will. I promise."

After we hung up I sat on the bed, staring at the wall and replaying the conversation. There had been no panic or concern in her voice, only aggravation with the manager at the post office. Maybe she was right and there was nothing to worry about. I didn't see it at the time, but I am sure she was frightened. Like me, anger was a far easier emotion for her to express than fear, and the manager at the post office gave her a perfect outlet for it. In the end, I figured, if she wasn't concerned, there was no reason for me to be either. I

Seeing Clearly

had a full day of sales calls planned with two of my colleagues who would be there to pick me up shortly. I finished getting dressed and headed downstairs to meet them, Renee and Bobbie, who were waiting in the car when I got there.

As we pulled away from the hotel there was the usual small talk about their weekends, their kids, and my flight from Atlanta. Finally one of them asked, "How's Holly? You must be getting excited. It's getting close!"

"She's okay, I think. I had a strange call from her this morning," I said. "She apparently stopped at the post office on the way to work and she said she thinks her water broke."

"WHAT?! Are you serious?" they asked in unison.

"Well, yeah. But she said she thought it was just a little and probably not a big deal. She is going to see her doctor a little later and said she would call me as soon as she knew more."

"Chris, you need to go home, now!" Before I knew it, we were on our way back to the hotel, and one of them was on the telephone with our travel department. It was no longer my decision. I was going home immediately.

Before we got to the hotel, they had me booked on the next flight out of DFW, which left in less than an hour. They followed me to my room and Renee started throwing my things into my suitcase while Bobbie called a friend of hers who was a gate agent at DFW and pleaded with her to do anything she could to hold the plane for me. While all that was going on, I called my wife to let her know what I was doing. Turns out that Holly had called her doctor and he told her to go immediately to the hospital, in fact the emergency room, not his office. It seems she was the only one who had not understood the severity of the situation.

I sprinted through the airport. Thank God this was prior to 9/11 and security was so much easier in those days. As the gate area came into view my heart sank. It was deserted. It was too late.

I had missed the flight. Then I heard a woman shout out, "Are you the guy from Irving?"

"YES! That's me."

"Hurry! I held it as long as I could." She handed me my boarding pass. The airplane door closed behind me before I could sit down. She had also upgraded me to First Class. The flight attendant congratulated me and gave me a small bottle of champagne and then, all of a sudden, there was nothing I could do but sit and wait and think. Holly wasn't due for nearly six weeks. The last thing I heard was that she was headed to the emergency room.

What am I flying home to?

As much as I tried to focus on all that could be going right in Atlanta, my mind kept jumping to all that could be going wrong. I would try to picture Holly and myself smiling and holding our newborn baby, but as soon as that image entered my consciousness it was immediately wiped out by one horrible scenario after another. That is how my mind has always worked. It's clearly a defense mechanism, helping me to be prepared for the worst possible scenario.

I hated the thought of being seen as emotional or out of control. Not only would crying in front of others have been embarrassing, it would have made me feel like that scared little boy whom I had worked so hard to ignore. I am not so naive as to say that is no longer the case, but I am far more aware of how I tend to stifle my emotions, and today I try to pay more attention to what my heart is telling me. But on that day in 1994, I would have done anything to stay in control of my emotions, or more precisely, to be seen as being in control of them.

My flight from Dallas was less than three hours. It felt like twice that. It was sometime after 4:00 in the afternoon when I finally got to the hospital. I could see the relief on Holly's face as soon as I walked in the door. I was happy and relieved to see my wife so amazingly calm and relaxed. It seemed as though none of the horrible outcomes I had imagined on my flight ever crossed her mind. If they did, she kept it to herself, but then, like me, she would have wanted to be in control of her emotions as well, so it's hard for me to say for sure. I have no memory of ever discussing it with her.

The doctor came in to check on Holly. "Hey, you made it," he said when he saw me. "I heard you had a crazy day."

"Yeah, but probably nothing like my wife's. How is she? How's the baby?"

"Everybody's fine. She's having intermittent mild contractions and she is only partially dilated. It is probably going to be a while. She may not even have the baby today, which is for the best. Every day makes a difference. If you want, you could run home for a bit. I am sure it will be hours at least, maybe even days."

It was amazing how at ease everyone was. Everything seemed so routine. I finally began to relax for the first time since my phone call with Holly that morning.

"Okay, thanks. Maybe later. Right now, I think I will stay here with her for a bit."

Holly had apparently decided she would not have the baby until I got there, and she didn't, but it wasn't long after that conversation before everything changed. Before I knew it, her contractions started coming fast and hard. Things happened so quickly. It was 5:13 p.m., only an hour after I had walked into the room, when the doctor announced, "You have a beautiful baby boy!" Thank God I had not taken the doctor's advice and gone home for a shower or something to eat.

When I heard my son cry, all the panic and fear melted away. All I felt was the excitement and joy of seeing my son come into the world. It was no longer just Holly and me. We were no longer just a couple; we were a family. Holly was right—everything had turned out fine after all.

Then, for the first time, I noticed that there were two or three other medical professionals off to the side with a small cart with several medical devices attached to it. *Where did they come from?* I had not seen them enter the room. I could see that my son was lying on the cart and that they were doing something with him, although I could not see what. I only noticed that there seemed to be some sense of urgency with whatever it was. The delivery room we were in was a large one, but it suddenly felt crowded with people in varying colors of scrubs.

Is this normal? Maybe they are just cleaning him up.

Instinctively, I knew that there was a problem. Something was terribly wrong. I felt my chest tighten as I watched, listening for any clues as to what was happening. After a minute or two they brought him over and laid him briefly on Holly's chest.

"How is he?" I asked.

"He likes the oxygen," was the answer, and before either of us knew it, with no further explanation, they were gone and so was our son.

"What's going on?" I asked the doctor. "Is he okay? Where are they taking him? Who are those people?"

"They are respiratory therapists. They are just going to check him out. Let's just get your wife taken care of and then we will find out more."

It took an hour or so before we found out that he had been sent to the Neonatal Intensive Care Unit (NICU). When we finally saw him, he had a clear, plexiglass oxygen hood over his head and his chest was heaving like he had just run a marathon. He was long and lean—twenty inches and five pounds, twelve ounces. Above his head hung a small handwritten sign on baby blue paper: "Baby Boy Monnette." There he was, fighting for his life, and he didn't even have a name. We had talked about names for our baby frequently over the last several months; we just thought we had six more weeks to decide. We named him Jonathan Alan and had them replace the sign with his name.

Sometime before midnight, the doctor sent me home. Holly needed to sleep and there was nothing anyone could do for Jonathan but wait. The house was dark and empty, just me and the dogs. Scattered around were a few partially filled cardboard boxes. *Shit. The movers.* We had already sold our home, and in just a few weeks we were supposed to be five hundred miles away in Cincinnati. I felt rage boiling up inside me. This was all Holly's fault! "Goddammit, Holly," I shouted to no one in particular! "Why the hell did we have to wait till the last minute?" What was happening with Jonathan wasn't her fault, but at that moment it didn't matter. As with Holly's experience at the post office that morning, all the fear I felt boiled over as anger. I took a few breaths to calm myself. I was exhausted. The house and the movers would just have to wait.

I poured myself a bourbon to try and celebrate my son's birth. I sat on the couch in the living room. The only light was what spilled in from the kitchen where I had entered the house. I sat there, alone in the dark, trying to feel the joy of being a new father, but all I could see was the image of Jonathan lying in the NICU gasping for breath. Everything was going terribly wrong. I was frightened. *What if he doesn't survive? What will I be walking into when I return to the hospital in the morning?*

I closed my eyes and prayed, "God, please let our son live." I could no longer hold back the tears and, for the first time in my adult life, I began to sob. I felt so helpless and scared, and crying only made everything feel worse, but the more I tried to stop the tears the harder I seemed to cry. *Whoever said crying makes you feel better is full of shit*, I thought. I am sure that had I been anywhere other than home alone in the dark that night I would never have allowed myself that moment of weakness. It would be more than a decade before I would cry like that again.

I am not sure what was going on with Holly in her hospital

room that evening while I sat alone on our couch at home crying. I have no memory of us discussing it beyond, "Did you get any sleep?" I imagine she too was overwhelmed by emotion, but she did not have the same privacy as me. Nurses were in and out of her room throughout the night, so she might not have felt safe in showing such emotion.

We were in Holly's hospital room the next morning when we first met the doctor, a neonatal specialist, who was charged with our son's care.

"How is our son?" we asked.

He paused briefly, then he looked down and slowly shook his head. "Jonathan is a very sick little boy."

I had hoped to hear things were not as bad as I had feared the night before, but in an instant, it was clear that was not the case. "He will be all right, won't he? I mean, he isn't going to die?"

I will never forget his answer. "John F. Kennedy's son died from the same thing."

I can think of a hundred different ways he could have answered my question. Instead, his message was that one of the most powerful men in the world from one of the wealthiest families did not have the resources to save their child. If his intent was to scare us, it worked, and we found little comfort as he walked us through the details.

Jonathan's lungs had not fully developed so they were like a new balloon that had never been inflated. He had to work hard with each breath just to fill his lungs with air, a condition known as respiratory distress syndrome. With all of his struggling to breathe, somewhere in the middle of the night he had torn a small hole in his right lung so, like a balloon with a hole, it collapsed—a pneumothorax. They inserted another tube through a small incision in his chest that drained fluid into a jar, somehow allowing the lung to properly inflate. To relieve the tremendous stress of fighting for each breath they had also intubated him, running a tube down his throat so a machine could pump in oxygen and pump out carbon dioxide—and that meant he had to be sedated.

With the tube in his throat providing the air he needed to stay alive, he had to be fed by another tube that went through his nose and into his stomach, where they would inject breast milk several times a day. He had an IV in the top of his head, at the fontanelle, where there is a gap in the skull allowing his head to compress sightly during childbirth. He had a pulse-ox sensor on his finger and two or three wires connected to an ECG to measure his heart's electrical activity. When we saw him that morning, lying there sedated with all the wires and tubes connected to him, he looked more like a lab experiment than our precious newborn baby.

Jonathan was small, but he was one of the largest by far in the NICU. There were several babies who were half the weight of our son. Babies who had been born far earlier than thirty-four weeks. Their hands so tiny and frail that I doubt their fingers would be able to wrap completely around my finger if they were to hold it.

In one isolated room lay a young boy much larger than our son. On every visit we made to the NICU, we would hear alarms going off in his room and see doctors and nurses run in to attend to him urgently. It seemed as though he was fighting for his life on a daily basis. Just like Jonathan, he too had his name printed on a baby blue card. His name was Josh, and around his room were dozens of balloons and cards celebrating his birthday. Josh had been in the NICU for a year and from what I could tell, he would not be leaving anytime soon. The thought horrified me. What did that poor little child have to look forward to in this world? His memory would stay with me for the rest of my life.

Somewhere during those first two weeks the movers came to our house, packed up all of our belongings, loaded them on a truck, and headed north to Cincinnati. I know I was there the day they loaded the truck, but it is mostly a blur.

The first week or two of Jonathan's life were filled with challenges, but then things started to get better. They removed the chest tube, then the breathing tube. The feeding tube was the last one to go, and it took him a week or so to learn to eat. By the time he was discharged, Jonathan had spent three weeks in the hospital, most of that time in the Neonatal Intensive Care Unit. Today he is a healthy and happy adult whom we could not be more proud of.

Back in August 1994, when Jonathan was fighting for his life in the NICU, all I could see was what could go wrong. It was hard for me to visualize things working out as well as they did. At that same time, I had no doubt that Holly and I would spend the rest of our lives together. Why is it that one was so hard to imagine and the other so easy, and yet, I would eventually be so wrong about both?

The fears I felt about my son's future were probably reasonable given all the information available to us at the time. Certainly, the doctor had made that abundantly clear with his reference to the tragedy the Kennedy family had experienced.

The challenges Holly and I faced were far more subtle and easier to ignore, but the warning signs were there from the beginning. Neither of us had any fluency in the language of emotions. I won't be so arrogant as to suggest I know why that was the case for Holly, but for me it was because I didn't know how to be vulnerable with the one person in my life with whom I should have felt the safest doing so: my wife.

9

The Beginning of an End

When Holly and I left the Washington, DC area, we were looking for a community where we could settle down and start a family, but our stay in Atlanta had been far too brief for that. Cincinnati was just what we were looking for. We had a comfortable home in a quiet and safe neighborhood in the suburbs, we were surrounded by families with young children, and with Holly's family just an hour and a half away, it felt like the perfect place to raise a family.

About a year and a half later we got the great news that Holly was once again pregnant. Holly discussed Jonathan's premature birth with her doctor; we clearly didn't want a repeat of the same situation with this pregnancy. The doctor told her that there was little they could do to prevent her from going into labor prematurely. At least this time they knew to watch out for possible warnings signs, and given Holly's "advanced maternal age" of thirty-seven, she also suggested that they do an amniocentesis test. The amnio is a procedure that involves withdrawing a sample of the amniotic fluid from her uterus. This allows the doctor to check for a variety of things such as genetic abnormalities, paternity testing, and even to determine if the baby's lungs are developed enough for birth.

A week or so later the doctor called with the results of the test. We were in our bedroom when Holly answered the phone. I could tell almost immediately by the look on Holly's face that something was wrong. She put the call on speakerphone, and we sat on the bed and listened as the doctor shared the news. The test had identified a "genetic abnormality," which would impact the development of the fetus. There was no surgery, no drug, no treatment of any kind that could correct whatever was wrong. We would not know the extent of its effect until the baby was born. I remember Holly and me sitting on the bed listening as the doctor walked us through the facts.

"There is no way of telling how severely handicapped your child will be. It could be mild, or it could be so severe that your baby may not even survive, but there is no doubt that there will be some complications, probably for the rest of your child's life."

"I will let you think about what you want to do," she said.

There were only two options we had to choose from. We would have the baby, or we would "terminate" the pregnancy. I remember thinking what a sterile word that was. As if we could just change our mind and move on as if we had terminated a lease on an apartment.

After we hung up, we sat there and looked at each other, both lost in our own thoughts. How could we possibly consider an abortion, particularly since we had no idea how severe the situation might be? The doctor had said that any handicap our child would have could potentially be minimal. Wasn't that a chance worth taking? But then there was Josh back in the NICU in Atlanta. Jonathan's birth was scary, but the complications he faced had only lasted a few weeks and everything turned out fine in the end. Josh had already been there a year when Jonathan was born, and he was fighting for his life every single day. He would be more than two years old by now. What was his life like today?

Seeing Clearly

What kind of a future would he have, if he even had one?

Do I have the strength to go through that? Am I really that weak?

I wish I knew what was in Holly's heart at that time, but I have no memory of discussing it with her. We talked about the facts, the options, and what we should do. I can imagine that, like me, she felt tremendous sorrow and loss. I wonder if there was some sort of feeling of failure as well. She had not carried Jonathan to full term, and we had almost lost him—now this. I never saw it as anyone's failure, certainly not Holly's. If anyone carried some sort of genetic material that might impact a healthy pregnancy it would be easy to make a connection through me back to my mother, but I have no reason to believe it was anything more than fate. Whatever she was feeling at the time, I sensed it was deeply personal and probably something that would be difficult for me to understand on my own. I can imagine there may have been a similar feeling in my mother's heart with all the miscarriages as well, but I never discussed it with her either.

Holly was clear with me that whatever decision we made, it would be made together. While I appreciated that, in my mind the final decision had to be hers. It was her body, and while I might have some input into her decision, she would be the one that would sign the consent forms, she would be the one to lie on the table while they performed the procedure, and she would be the one who would carry those vivid memories for the rest of her life. I would simply sit in a sterile waiting room while all that happened.

At one point, Holly asked, "If it were you, would you want to live that life?"

It would have been easy to answer "no" to that as a hypothetical question. It was a lot harder to answer that same question about the unborn child she was carrying at the time. On one hand, we had a beautiful son who'd had a very rocky start in life, and everything turned out great in the end. He was healthy and happy with a bright future before him. On the other hand, there was Josh.

I don't know if I ever shared with her just how terrified I was with either option. I am fairly sure I never told her that my biggest fear was that I wasn't strong enough, emotionally, to raise a child with, potentially, significant special needs. It seemed so "weak" and I was embarrassed that I felt that way.

In the end, my answer to her question was that, regardless of how I felt it might impact our lives, I could not imagine wanting to live the life that Josh had, but I would support whatever she wanted to do. Today, I cannot tell you what my opinion on abortion was before we were forced to consider such a choice. I am certain that neither of us would have considered it as strictly an alternative to birth control, but this was so much more complex.

I wonder how many of those people standing outside the abortion clinic that day, screaming insults at us as we walked inside, were ever faced with such a decision? The pain in my wife's eyes was palpable and it broke my heart. We shared at least one feeling in common with the protestors: We both wanted nothing more than for us to be somewhere else that day. I loved my wife and as I saw her pain I wanted to run over and confront them directly. Someone had to be to blame for this and at that point, I wanted it to be them.

There is no way I will ever forget the deep sadness on Holly's face as she walked out. I searched for the right words to help ease her pain, but all I could do was ask, "How are you?"

Her reply was simply, "I just want to go home."

After that day, there was little discussion of the abortion except to talk about her physical recovery in the days that followed. When that was behind us, it was never mentioned between us again. Not even once, that I can recall, in the twenty-five years since that day. It's as if we just pressed delete and the memory was gone. It's such a telling example of how we both dealt with painful emotions. We turned inward, which put distance between us, rather than pulling

Seeing Clearly

us together. There are so many examples in my life of me turning my back on painful memories, but that one shocks me to this day. There could not have been a bigger warning sign of trouble ahead for us than that, but we never saw it.

Given all that had happened with our first two pregnancies, it is somewhat surprising to me, in hindsight, that we decided to try again. It would have been easy to just give up, but we really wanted a second child, and I am so glad we did. Less than a year later, Holly was again pregnant. This time, everything went flawlessly. Our daughter, Jennifer, came into the world on August 29, 1997, our fifth wedding anniversary, exactly seven years after our first date, and six days after her brother's third birthday. Her birth was uneventful, if you can say that about the birth of any child. I had always heard about the bond between fathers and daughters, but to experience it is a different thing altogether. It's not that I loved her more than my son. That was impossible. It was just somehow different—special.

Today, I sometimes wonder if there isn't some similarity to my own birth and the relationship with my mother. I was born following a lot of adversity in my parents' lives, and I think that might have led my mother to cling to me just a bit tighter. Perhaps that was also at play with Jen's birth. I am my mother's son after all, and there is no doubt that Holly and I had our own adversity leading up to Jennifer's birth.

Life didn't slow down for us after Jennifer's birth. From the time Holly and I were married we had been searching for a place that we could call home, but every time we thought we found it, the moving trucks would show up, and Cincinnati would be no different.

Only three months after Jennifer was born, I was offered my third promotion in as many years. This time the promotion would require a move to Toronto, where I was tasked with rebuilding our floundering sales and marketing operation in Canada. It remains, to this day, the best job I've ever had. I was blessed with an amazing team who were more friends than co-workers, and together, for three straight years, we grew that business at an incredible rate, blowing away every revenue target the company gave us. I could not help but reflect back on the decision I had made more than ten years earlier to pursue a career in sales. I had not failed, as Kathleen had suggested; rather, I had thrived and my confidence in myself was growing with each success.

I loved everything about that job. If it had been strictly my choice, I could have stayed there forever, but Holly and I were US citizens. I had a work visa, but Holly didn't, and at the time she expressed a desire to get back into the job market. That meant we had to leave Canada, so when I heard from a colleague in California that she was looking for a business leader for our customer support operation based out of Eugene, Oregon, I raised my hand. In March 2000 I accepted the last promotion I would receive during my tenure with that company, and we packed up once again and headed to Eugene.

Atlanta had lasted only eighteen months. Cincinnati was promising but three years later we were gone. As a US citizen, Canada was always temporary. Eugene was a small community where it was easy to get to know everyone and almost instantly it felt like home. I was forty-one when we moved to Eugene, and it was the first place I seriously thought I would spend the rest of my life.

We bought a beautiful home in the south hills overlooking the Willamette Valley, our kids were in a private school at the bottom of the hill, and we had a growing investment account that promised a comfortable retirement, thanks to several promotions and the strong performance of my company's stock.

It had always been a dream of mine to own a small airplane. I got my private pilot's license in Cincinnati in the summer of 1995,

Seeing Clearly

but we never had the money to buy a plane. Eight years later our financial situation was better. In February 2003, we found a Cessna 182 for sale in San Jose and decided, why not? It had just enough range to carry the four of us down to California to see her brother, who had a home near Groveland. WE could get to the wine country in California, or up to Seattle. It was the perfect extravagance for us.

For me, the plane served a couple of purposes. It was like meditation. When I was flying, I was rarely thinking of anything else except flying the airplane, navigating, making sure the engine was performing as expected, the weather, and talking to air traffic control. There was no room for whatever troubles I may have been dealing with at work or any disagreements I may have had with my wife. It was a wonderful escape.

While I would never have said as much at the time, looking back, I think the idea of owning an airplane was also some sort of a capstone. A symbol that I had achieved some level of success. As it turned out, it was also a symbol of a dramatic turning point in our lives and the first shoe would drop almost instantly.

On Valentine's Day, I flew down to San Jose with a sizable check in my pocket to pick up our new plane and fly home. About an hour before I was to pick up the plane, my cell phone rang. It was my boss.

"Chris, got a few minutes to chat?"

"Sure, Steve, what's up?"

"Before we get started, you need to know that I have Kerre from HR on the phone with me." Suddenly I knew that everything was about the change. "Listen, I am just gonna give it to you straight, Chris. We are eliminating your position."

The call from my boss was predictable. At the direction of our CFO, I had led a project to investigate the financial benefit of outsourcing my customer support operation. We had spent months dispassionately investigating it with multiple outsourcing providers and ultimately determined that it would be far more expensive than keeping the operation in-house. Our CFO's response showed we had clearly given him the wrong answer. "Listen, if you don't want to do this, I can get somebody who will! Now go back and rework those numbers and show me how this makes sense." I have always believed that numbers don't lie, but what I have learned over the years is that you can frequently use the same data to reinforce a variety of positions. We rearranged the numbers on the spreadsheet and came back with a more compelling financial analysis in-hand.

So, just a few months before my conversation with my boss, I had personally delivered the same message to hundreds of people. I vividly remember standing in front of one crowded room telling them that their jobs had been eliminated. Seated in the front row, directly in front of me, sat a young woman who had just returned from maternity leave that day. Tears were streaming down her face. I imagine I came across as an uncaring corporate "suit" whose only concern was the corporate profits. In fact, I believe at least a few people told me as much. I can see how my need to be in control of my emotions would have resulted in me sounding flat and uncaring. If I were a woman, I imagine they might have used the same term my customer had used for Holly the day I met her. What no one saw was how I sat in my car shaking, with my eyes filled with tears after I walked out of the room that day. I knew just how much pain I had caused. It wasn't my decision, but it was my responsibility to deliver the blow.

As my boss and the director of HR laid out my own personal severance plan, I knew that the decision wasn't Steve's. He too was the messenger. I had expected that my role would change, and I had known there was a chance I could get laid off, but I had been rather naive. For more than a decade I had delivered repeatedly on every challenge the company presented to me. So many of my personal relationships, my net worth, and much of my personal identity were tied to the company. Getting laid off was a huge emotional blow to

Seeing Clearly

me. It was also the first big blow to my career. In an instant, a future that had been so clear to me was suddenly blurry and hard to see.

I called Holly and told her the news. "Should I just catch a United flight home and forget about buying the airplane?"

She thought about it for a minute. "No! Screw them. They can't keep us down. Go get our airplane. I'll see you when you get home."

Had I known the path in front of me at the time, I would have left the check in my pocket and caught the next United flight home, but instead I handed over the check and flew home in our airplane to an uncertain future.

Losing my job, along with all that I had tied up in that company, was painful, particularly because it felt as if I had been used. I had been forced to be the "hatchet man," firing hundreds of people before receiving the same fate. My attitude at the time was, "Fuck them! I'll just find a better job." As I was suddenly faced with the prospect of looking for a new job for the first time in more than a decade, I had a surprising sense of self-confidence, which seems odd given how much I had struggled with it for most of my life. Today, I am not sure if that was my confidence or my determination to show everyone just what a mistake the company made by letting me go. At the time, I am certain I would have said it was confidence.

I spent several months looking for a job, and suddenly the small-town environment was far less attractive. There were jobs, but nothing that would replace the income I had lost. Any comparable job would almost certainly mean yet another move and that was the last thing we wanted to do. Rather than leave our home in Eugene I started looking at entrepreneurial opportunities. If I couldn't find a job, I'd just create one! We looked at a variety of small businesses that I had heard might be for sale. Most were either way out of reach financially or completely unappealing.

Along the way a friend and former boss approached me with an interesting startup opportunity. He was a partner in a venture capital firm. His firm had given a local coffee roaster $70,000 to fund the research and development of an interesting new coffee drink. The product never came to market, and it was tied up in a dispute between the two parties. He knew me from the years we had worked together and thought that I could help them resolve the dispute and ultimately bring the product to market. If I could put the deal together with the coffee roaster, they would give me their interest in the intellectual property for a small stake in the business. I was intrigued by the idea, and the confidence my former boss had in my abilities to be successful was compelling as well.

The patent-pending process allowed botanical extracts, such as echinacea or ginseng, to be infused into coffee beans during the roasting process. Coffee as a health drink was certainly a new idea, and as I began to research the opportunity, it became clear there could be a huge market for it. Coffee was the second most traded commodity in the world. Only oil was larger. Americans drink more than 400 million cups of coffee a day! At the time, everywhere you turned you would see new "healthy" beverages—herbal teas, kombucha, vitamin waters—even Anheuser-Busch had a beer infused with ginseng. It was an explosive market, so why wouldn't one of the most popular beverages in the country be a great option? Herbal teas were already huge, and coffee didn't seem like that big of a stretch to me. Even a tiny piece of the market would be a great business. In the end I said yes, and we created Caffe Botanica, which would turn out to be my second, and by far largest, career failure.

We created three products: ENERGY, a Swiss Water decaffeinated coffee infused with Asian ginseng; STRENGTH, infused with calcium; and HEALTH, infused with echinacea, which is believed to boost your immune system and, in an interesting twist of fate, your eyesight. Of the three, HEALTH was my favorite by far, although it apparently did little for my eyesight.

Seeing Clearly

I recruited a great board of directors including the founder of two major, well-known tea brands, and the former CEO of a major national food company. The coffee was excellent, the market was there, and the branding was beautiful, but the execution was far from flawless. I seriously underestimated what it would take to get the business off the ground, particularly since I had no domain expertise in the food and beverage industry. I knew little about manufacturing, my knowledge of coffee was that of a consumer, and botanical extracts were little more than a mystery to me. I had to learn everything from scratch.

By the summer of 2004 it had been more than a year since I'd had a paying job and there was little sign that our business would replace my lost income anytime in the near future. Not only had we been living off our savings, but we had been investing money into the business at an unsustainable rate. The prospect of our coffee business paying our mortgage and living expenses before we ran out of savings was beginning to seem unlikely. So, not only was I failing miserably, I was also jeopardizing our entire future in the process. Whatever confidence I felt as we were starting the business was gone, and all I could feel was the pending failure. I had finally stepped off a ledge too high for me to handle. It was, unquestionably, the lowest part of my career, at least to that point.

That's when the next shoe dropped. Like the last one, this one started with a phone call as well. This time it was my father. I can probably count on one hand the number of times my father called me himself. So, when I answered the phone and heard his voice, I knew something was up.

"Dad? What's the matter?"

"Look, I don't think it is anything to worry about, but your mother was, well, acting a little funny, so we took her to the hospital. You know, just to be sure."

"Oh my god, Dad! Is she all right?"

"Yes, I think she'll be fine, but they are going to keep her here for a little bit."

"What happened?"

"They think she had a stroke, but she seems like she should be okay."

I was shaking, and my heart was pounding in my chest. I knew my father. He wouldn't let on just how bad it really was. "I am coming out. I will get the first flight out tomorrow."

"I really don't think you need to do that, Chris. Not yet. I will let you know when I hear more."

"Dad, I'll be there tomorrow."

And in an instant, my failing business no longer mattered.

10

Always

If there is any point in my life that I can look back on and clearly see the presence of that scared little boy my therapist and I discussed, it was in the days following my mother's stroke. Nothing in my life felt secure. My career was failing, taking with it our life's savings, and I was suddenly faced with the harsh reality that I could lose the one person who had always been there to pick me up whenever I fell: my mother. With each wave of bad news, it felt as though the ground below me was being washed away. I dropped everything and ran to Virginia to be with my parents. I think I was also running away from our crumbling financial future, although that was never a conscious thought.

Fortunately, as my father had indicated when he called, Mom was in much better shape than I had feared. She was doing well enough that she was released from the hospital not that long after I arrived. There was minimal cognitive impairment from the stroke; however, she did have some significant mobility issues. Mom had already been struggling with chronic obstructive pulmonary disease for years, the result of decades of smoking, but she had been able to get around on her own. The stroke robbed her of what little independence she had. She could use a walker for short distances, but anything more than walking across the room required a wheelchair. Making it up their steep stairs to her bedroom was impossible by herself and a risky proposition even with my help.

At seventy-nine Dad was ill equipped to take on the challenge of being her sole caretaker. Over the years, they had become quite isolated, so there wasn't anybody nearby they could call on for help if they needed it. It was clear there was no way I could leave them in Virginia by themselves. Holly and I had plenty of space in our house and could help Mom with her recovery. I knew Mom would be okay with it. She missed seeing her grandchildren, so being near them would be a huge plus for her. The issue would be with my father. I could hear his words in my head: "I appreciate that, Chris, but no, we will be fine right here. We can't just pack up and move to the other side of the country. This is our home. Don't worry, we will be okay."

To my complete surprise his answer was, "We would love that. Thank you." He must have felt extremely vulnerable to jump at that offer without so much as a question. Once that decision was made, things happened quickly. We put their house on the market, and, thanks to my father's meticulous care over the twenty years they had lived there, it sold in a matter of days, so only a few weeks after Mom's stroke they were in our home in Oregon.

When I got back to Oregon with my parents, our coffee business remained on the back burner for me. As much as I knew that I needed to be spending every waking moment focused on keeping the business alive, I had lost whatever drive I had to make it successful. All I could focus on was my mother's health and getting both of my parents settled down in their new home in Oregon. I would guess that my mother's health also helped me justify what was happening with our business, a balm of sorts for my damaged ego: "The failure wasn't my fault. I had to be there for Mom." It was most likely already too late to save the business, and my lack of commitment to saving it only ensured the outcome.

There was a silver lining in all that was happening. The distance that I had always felt between my father and me began to close. I have heard that adversity brings people closer, but that wasn't what I experienced with Holly over the years. If anything, with each difficult chapter in our life, we pulled apart as we retreated into ourselves.

My father was never a man to show a lot of emotions, but as he watched what was happening with the woman he had shared his life with since the day he met her in 1943, I saw a vulnerability in him that I had never seen before. He wasn't a giant whom I could never measure up to; he was just a man. As I look back on those days, the love I feel in my heart for my father is overwhelming, but at the time, I couldn't express it to him, yet our relationship grew closer than I could have ever imagined.

That isn't to say we didn't have our share of disagreements and challenges. Particularly when it came to Mom's care. I was a stickler for the rules. I thought that if we were diligent in following the doctor's orders things would get back to the way they were. Dad's focus was on making his wife happy. Today, knowing how things turned out, I wish I'd had the same focus as he did. For as long as I can remember, when they were living in their home in Virginia, just before dinnertime, Dad would announce, "Julanne, I am going to have a cocktail. Would you like one?"

She would answer, "Ooh, that would be great."

He would return a few minutes later with a Manhattan for himself and a gin martini for my mother. After the stroke, one of the doctor's orders was for my mother to abstain from drinking alcohol, yet every night I would see Dad bring Mom a martini, and every night I would say, "Dad, what are you doing? You know she isn't supposed to have any alcohol."

"It's just one drink, Chris! It isn't going to kill her."

"You don't know that and besides, I am not the one saying that. It's the doctor!"

"For God's sake, Chris, it's one watered-down martini."

"But Dad…"

"Goddamn it, Chris! She has been through a lot, and if my wife wants a martini, I am going to give her one!" And that was exactly what he would do. As much as I know my father loved his children, neither Mike nor I had quite the same status in his eyes as our mother. My father made that painfully clear to me one day when I was a teenager. My mother and I had some disagreement, and I went to my father to ask him to overrule her decision. I will never forget his words. "That woman was in my life long before you or your brother came along and she will be the only one still here long after you have both moved on. Trust me, you don't want to ask me to make a choice between the two of you."

I was shocked. I was hurt. How could he say that to me? I was his son! Today, I see it so differently and it makes me smile. He adored my mother, and she deserved every bit of that. She was an amazing woman who meant the world to both of us. As he would demonstrate over the next few months, those were not just words. She was truly everything to him.

One day in October, about a month after my parents had moved into our home in Oregon, Holly called me at the office.

"Chris, you better come."

"Why? What's going on?"

"It's your mother. She is acting strange, and she keeps asking for you. Just hurry up and get here."

"Okay. I will be there in fifteen minutes."

When I walked into the living room Mom was sitting in her

Seeing Clearly

wheelchair next to the fireplace. Dad was sitting in a chair next to her. He was holding her hand and seemed to be pleading with her.

"Oh, come on, Julie. Don't say that. You know me."

"Get away from me!" And she tried to pull her arm away, but Dad just held on.

I came over to where they were sitting and my father looked up to me, almost pleading for help, and then just stepped back. He stood a few feet away, watching, awkwardly. Shaking. I could see he was close to tears.

I took my father's seat and sat next to her with my hand gently on her arm.

"It's okay, Mom. What's going on?"

"I am glad you are here," she said. "Who is this guy? He just keeps touching me. I think he's a pervert."

"Mom, you know who that is. That's your husband, Jerry. My father."

"I have never seen him before. Tell him to stay away from me."

If I hadn't seen the pain in my father's eyes, I might have laughed out loud. There was an odd sense of irony to what was happening. It was not that different than when her mother-in-law, my grandmother, had temporarily lived with us over thirty years before. I could suddenly hear my grandmother's words: "Bud, who is this strange woman in the house?"

As I sat across from my mother, I noticed a slight paralysis on one side of her face, and I knew in an instant what was happening. She was having another stroke.

Oh God no! Please not another one.

"Mom, you are having a stroke. I need to get you to the hospital right away!"

"I am not going to the hospital," she insisted. "I am fine. Just get that man away from me!"

"Yes, you are going, Mom. Right now!"

While she complained loudly about it, I forced her into our car. I needed to get her to the hospital immediately.

As she fought me, she bumped her head on the door jamb while trying to keep from getting in the car.

"What the hell are you doing to me? You can't treat me this way. I am going to call the police," she protested.

"I am sorry, Mom. It was an accident. I just need to get you to the hospital."

As we pulled away from the house that night, the thought never occurred to me that it would be her last time in our home. I just needed to get her to the hospital, and everything would be fine again. Just as it always was.

She complained loudly the whole way.

"How could you treat me that way?"

We pulled up in front of the hospital and again I had to forcibly remove her from the car. As we entered the emergency room the nurse on duty noticed the commotion and asked what was going on.

"He is abusing me. He slammed my head into the car while he was forcing me into it. Tell him to leave me alone!" my mother demanded.

The nurse looked at me immediately. It was obvious she was trying to make a judgment call as to whether I might have done something to her.

"I think my mother is having a stroke. She has already had one."

The nurse turned her attention again to my mother.

"Stick out your tongue."

Mom complied and stuck out her tongue. It immediately went to one side.

"Take my hands and squeeze them both at the same time."

Again, Mom complied.

The nurse looked at me for a moment, then picked up the phone

Seeing Clearly

and said only a few words. Within seconds my mother was whisked away into an examination room.

The second stroke was far worse than the first, or maybe it was the cumulative effect of the two. Whichever the case, she quickly deteriorated and before long, a day or two at most, she had become just a shell of who she once was. She lay in the bed staring aimlessly around the room, unable to communicate in any fashion.

The doctor offered little hope for recovery this time and, as if to underscore that point, after my brother and his wife flew up from Texas, he suggested that we all meet to discuss our mother's wishes. It was a somber meeting that started with him asking whether she would want them to attempt to resuscitate her if she stopped breathing or her heart stopped beating. The DNR order was clear. Mom had always been very specific about that. Then the questions got harder.

"If it is determined that she needs emergency surgery to save her life, should we do that or just keep her comfortable with painkillers?" he asked.

Dad said, "She wouldn't want surgery." The doctor added that to the chart.

"What if she develops a serious illness such as pneumonia, or an infection. Should we treat her with antibiotics?"

"Well maybe. I don't want her to suffer."

"We could keep her comfortable with pain medication," the doctor assured him.

"Well, I…I think you give her the antibiotics."

"Very well, Mr. Monnette." The doctor made another note.

"What if we are unable to feed her? Should we use a feeding tube?"

"My God, are you asking me to let my wife starve to death?"

"I assure you, we will make sure she is comfortable."

He looked down at his feet and answered quietly, "She wouldn't want to be fed through a tube."

The list seemed to go on and on, with each choice harder than the last. As we sat there making decisions on how to let my mother die, I could feel emotions building inside me like a pot about to boil over. I did everything I could to focus on the facts and not the implication of each decision. My father seemed to get older and more frail right before my eyes. By the time we left that room, there was no doubt where this was going. She would not be coming home, ever.

Mom was transferred to Valley West, a long-term care facility on the other side of town. For the next three months, every morning my father would get up, get dressed, have coffee and breakfast. Then he would drive across town and sit next to her bed. He would spend the day reading the paper to her, talking to her about whatever television show was on in her room, or sharing stories about things that were happening back at home with Holly, the kids, or me. It is hard to say what she understood, if anything. She would occasionally look at whoever was speaking or grunt some completely unintelligible sound. She seemed lost in a world that none of us had any access to. There was no sign of any comprehension, yet day in and day out Dad sat by her bed and talked to her as if she understood every word.

I am not completely sure how much of that was for him and how much of that he did for her. My father was an extremely disciplined man, and he loved his wife more than anything. His life had revolved around her from the day he met her nearly sixty years before. He wouldn't miss a day, and I couldn't imagine him doing anything different.

Seeing Clearly

On January 20, 2005, one week after my forty-sixth birthday, I came home from work to find my dad sitting in his room watching TV, his Manhattan on the end table next to his recliner. I sat down in the adjacent recliner on my father's right. Mom's seat.

"How's Mom?"

"The same. She just lies there. I don't know if she even knows I'm in the room. It's just so goddamn hard to see her that way. I just don't know what to do."

"She knows you are there, Dad, and it makes a difference. Maybe she can't say so, but she knows."

"I don't know. Maybe."

We sat quietly for a few minutes watching TV together.

Then he added, "Something kinda strange happened, though, as I was getting ready to leave."

"What happened, Dad?"

"I was sitting there next to her and said, 'Okay, Julie, I am going to head home for dinner. I'll see you in the morning,' and she turned and looked right at me and smiled."

"See, Dad. She knows you were there."

"I guess." We sat quietly for a moment before he added, "Then she reached up with her hand and patted me on my cheek."

"Wow! Really?"

"Yeah. It was like she was trying to tell me something."

"She probably was, Dad. I think she was trying to tell you that she loved you and everything is going to be okay."

"Maybe," he said softly.

When the phone rang around 2 a.m., I knew before I answered it what my mother had been trying to tell my father. She was saying goodbye.

I spoke to the nurse for only a moment, told her we would be right over, and then I hung up.

I could see Holly searching my face to get a sense of what I was feeling. "Oh, I am so sorry, sweetie," she said. It would have been impossible for her to know what I was feeling. I didn't have a clue myself. I was numb.

"Yeah. Well, I guess we knew this was coming. I better wake up Dad." There was suddenly a lot to do, and I was in task mode. No time for tears now.

I walked downstairs to my father's room and knocked on his door. "Dad."

"Yes?"

"Valley West just called. It's Mom. She's gone."

After a long pause, "Okay. I'll be right out."

We drove over to the nursing home in silence. There was nothing to say.

As we walked toward her room I was surprised by just how dark and quiet the place was. I had been there numerous times over the last few months, and there had always been lots of activity. Families visiting. Nursing staff walking up and down the aisles pushing carts. Not tonight. Tonight, it had an eerie, vacant feeling. I didn't recognize the nursing staff, but they recognized Dad. He had been there every single day for three months.

"She is in her room," the woman at the front desk said softly.

Mom's room was dark. She had a roommate, but the curtain had been pulled between the two beds. I don't know if her roommate was there. I didn't look. All I could see was my mother, or at least her body. The sheets were pulled up as if she were asleep, but her mouth was wide open and there was a stillness I had never seen before. There wasn't the look of peace that I had expected to see. It was just emptiness.

My father walked over and tried to close her mouth. It immediately fell open again as soon as he removed his hand. He stood up, his face expressionless, and walked out of the room without a word.

Seeing Clearly

I stood there for a moment trying to figure out what to do. I didn't want to leave the room because I knew that when I did, she would be gone forever. Yet, as I looked at the completely vacant expression on her face, I knew she already was. I could feel a torrent of emotions just barely below the surface and I knew that if I stayed much longer, they would overcome me.

I leaned over, kissed her forehead, and said, "I love you, Mom." I stood up, turned toward the door, and stopped. On the other side of the doorway lay a life without my mother, and in the room lay only her vacant body. I didn't want to be in either place.

Keep it together, Chris. Dad needs you now.

I took a deep breath to compose myself, stood up straight, and walked out the door without looking back. I desperately wanted to, but what was the use. It would only cause me more pain and that would solve nothing. The thing I needed the most was to not feel the pain. I'd had a glimpse of what was just under the surface, and it was excruciating. I could not allow myself to feel that.

Dad was standing by himself in the darkened lobby. The nurses sat quietly behind the counter off to one side. The scene was nothing new to them. They instinctually knew that he just needed to be left to his own thoughts.

"Do you need anything from us?" I asked.

"No. We have already called the mortuary and they are on their way to pick her up. They will take care of everything."

"Okay. Well, then, thank you for all you did for my mother."

"Of course, Mr. Monnette, and I am so sorry for your loss."

I tried to say, "Thank you," but all I could do was nod.

I turned to face my father, and we walked out without saying a word to each other.

When we got to the car I said, "It's still early, Dad. There is no use going back to the house right now. I can't sleep and I don't want to wake the kids yet. Do you want to get something to eat?"

"Okay," he said. It was the only word he had spoken since I woke him up that morning.

I vividly remember the lighting as we walked into Denny's. I had been asleep when the call came in, we had left the house without turning on the lights, and the lights were off at the nursing home. The harsh lighting created a sterile atmosphere that seemed to say, "This isn't the place for a lot of emotions." There were only a couple of other people in the restaurant. There was a small group that appeared to be winding down from a long night of partying, and a few others who were either just finishing a late shift or starting an early one.

"Would you like a booth or do you want to sit at the counter?" the waitress asked.

"A booth, please," I answered. I wanted some privacy. Sitting at the counter just felt so exposed, but when we sat across from each other in the booth and made eye contact, I realized that this was worse. I had no idea what to say to my own father. It was as if I was sitting with a stranger. We both got lost in our menus, somehow avoiding any eye contact. I don't remember feeling sorrow or pain at the time, only hollow emptiness.

After several minutes I said, "I'll call Mike when we get home."

"Okay."

"No need waking him up now. It's an hour later in Texas and he should be getting up in a couple hours."

"Yeah," Dad added.

"I'll call the mortuary when they open. The owner is a friend. He'll take care of everything."

"Thanks."

We sat there quietly shuffling food around on our plates.

"I guess she's in a better place now," I said.

"Yeah. I guess so."

I remember thinking how devastated and heartbroken he must

Seeing Clearly

have felt. He had barely said a word since he first heard the news. He was clearly in a lot of pain, but he hadn't shed a tear. In fact, as I looked across the table, I struggled to read any emotion on his face. All I knew was that he needed me now. I had to help him get through this.

The irony of the situation is so clear to me today. I had shown no more emotion, no more pain than my father had. I too had not shed a single tear. While it may have been true that Dad needed me more than ever, it was equally true that I needed to be needed. It allowed me to stay in my head and focus on the tasks that had to be accomplished rather than my heart, which was overwhelmed with sorrow.

For all my life my father had been the rock of our family. He was a big man. Even bigger than his six-foot-two-inch frame. He always seemed to stand just a little taller and a little straighter with his head held high. But that morning as we left the Denny's his head was not as high and his shoulders were soft and rounded. A huge part of him had just died.

Mom died on Friday, January 21, 2005. Her memorial service was planned for the following Wednesday. When the funeral director asked if any of the family members would like to give a eulogy, both my father and I declined. I would have loved to do so, but I knew there was little chance of me getting through it without completely losing my composure.

Thankfully, my brother said he wanted to do it. I offered to put together the music for the service. They both loved music and I had such wonderful memories of hearing them playing in our home. I picked four songs that I thought would give those in attendance just a hint of who she was. "It's Not for Me to Say" by Johnny Mathis, "Ava Maria" by Luciano Pavarotti, the theme song from her favorite television show, "Northern Exposure," and finally, "Always" by Patsy Cline. It was their song. Dad would play it on the piano while she sang along shamelessly in her squeaky singing voice.

I was shocked just how many people attended that day. The small chapel was full. Every one of our friends and several colleagues from work were there. I sat in the front row with Holly to my right, Jonathan and Jennifer on my left. Then, for the first time since my mother's stroke, there was nothing left for me to do. There was no cross-country move to plan. No need to search for a long-term care facility. There were no funeral arrangements to be made. The music was set. And everyone was in their place. There was nothing to distract me from the pain I had been hiding from. The moment I heard the familiar soft piano intro to the Johnny Mathis song I could feel a wave of emotions welling up inside. By the time he sang the first line, "It's not for me to say you love me," I wasn't just crying, I was bawling. Everything came crashing down in a way I never experienced in my life. I could no longer hold back the tears. I had held them for too long and there was no stopping the wall of emotions that was overrunning me.

My brother had prepared a wonderful eulogy, but in the end, like Dad and me, he was too emotional to share it with everybody. His wife, Marilyn, read it on his behalf. His words were loving and reflective about all that our mother had done for our family. How her strength helped our father reach so far in his Navy career and how it had helped her sons find success and happiness. Mike wrote about her love for golf and how she would never give up, no matter how hot the weather or how bad her game was.

It was a moving and heartfelt description of all that our mother had given to our family. While Dad was always the one who roared the loudest, it was our mother's strength that held everything together. She was without question the cornerstone of our family.

I wish I'd had the strength to stand up and tell everyone just what a wonderful woman my mother was, but all I could feel at the time was overwhelming sorrow.

Seeing Clearly

The service ended with Patsy Cline's "Always."

More than fifteen years later, I still can't hear that song without feeling emotional. At times it is hard for me to know exactly what I am feeling. I can hear my therapist Chad's words echo in my mind. "That's okay. You don't have to know what you feel. Just let yourself feel whatever is there. You can't think your way through this, Chris. You have to feel your way."

When I hear Patsy Cline's recording of "Always," if I just sit and open my heart to whatever emotion comes to me, it is amazing how much love I can now feel intertwined with the sorrow. It's as if they are flip sides of the same coin. It makes so much sense to me now. It is the loss of the things that we care the most about that cause us the most pain. The temptation to run from feeling that sorrow is compelling, but what I can see clearly now is that it is impossible to escape the pain and still hold on to the love of what was lost.

11

A Great Teacher

STANDING WHERE I AM TODAY, I can look back at the years surrounding my mother's death and see what a dramatic turning point that time was in my life. Thanks to the perspective of time and a lot of self-reflection, I can look at those years and see the presence of many of the same challenges that I am faced with now. The biggest difference is that today, as my vision is slipping away, I can see more clearly the emotional forces that are pulling at me. I was completely blind to them fifteen years ago. In that way, macular degeneration has been a great teacher for me.

It was also about that time when the first indication of a potential problem with my eyes was noticed. During a routine eye exam, the doctor noticed some spotting on my retina and referred me to a specialist who conducted a fluorescein angiography, the same test Dr. Lalwani would use years later to confirm the neovascular macular degeneration diagnosis. At the time it was determined that the spots were nothing to be worried about. They were drusen, a yellow deposit under the retina that, by themselves, were nothing to be worried about, although he suggested that I keep an eye on it with regular ophthalmology examinations. Today we know that the presence of drusen is an early indication of macular degeneration.

Those appointments never happened and the next ophthalmologist I saw was Dr. Lalwani half a dozen years later, after my vision was already significantly compromised. I didn't intentionally skip those appointments. They simply got lost as my life fell apart. A regular ophthalmology appointment was just one more casualty of the midlife crisis that began just months after my mother passed away.

The reality is that there is no cure, but there was a potential that had I begun taking the daily supplements that Dr. Lalwani later prescribed, I may have been able to slow the progression of the disease. I will never know how my vision would be different today if I had done so, yet I cannot help but wonder if the simple addition of the supplements earlier in the progression of the disease would have prevented the wet macular degeneration and the need for injections. Or maybe it would have slowed the progression to a point that today I would still be able to drive a car and I wouldn't be looking at the prospect of walking away from a great career, this time because I no longer feel capable of performing to my own high expectations.

Like the drusen in my eyes, there were warning signs of what would happen in my personal life that were ignored as well. A therapist once told Holly and me after our marriage was all but over, "Neither of you knew just how much Holly loved you, Chris, until it was too late." I imagine Holly might have said that the inverse was true as well. Emotional intimacy was hard for us. I obviously cannot speak for Holly's experience, but I think back through the tough times with Jonathan's first few weeks, Holly's second pregnancy, the loss of my job, the failure of our business, and the death of my mother. I have not one memory of being vulnerable enough with Holly to share just how sad and frightened I felt.

The dictionary defines *vulnerability* as being "capable of or susceptible to being wounded or hurt," as well as being "open to moral attack, criticism, temptation, etc." Today, as my central vision narrows and it becomes harder and harder to see things clearly, I am literally becoming more "susceptible to being wounded or hurt." My vision loss has made me, literally, more vulnerable. The risk of a misstep, like my father's fateful last step, becomes more real each day. Yet as difficult as it is to accept the physical vulnerability that comes with low vision, it is the second definition, the fear of criticism, that I have always struggled with. The fear of being judged poorly, and specifically, weak, has always been one of my biggest challenges. It is why I found it so hard to be open with the pain of the loss of my mother, particularly in front of my father. It is the thing that I know I must learn to overcome, to embrace, if I want to experience any abundance in my life. And it is one of the biggest lessons I am learning from my low vision.

To illustrate how my vision loss is teaching me the power of vulnerability I need to start with an explanation of how I see the world around me. Most people who meet me have no sense of the challenges I face. There are no outward signs of my disability. I don't use a white cane, nor do I have a seeing-eye dog, but spend some time with me and the challenges become obvious. When asked to describe my vision, I usually start by saying that what we see with the macula is only the center ten degrees or so of our eyesight. That's roughly the equivalent of holding an eight-inch salad plate at arm's length. That is what is lost with macular degeneration. The peripheral vision, everything outside of that salad plate, is unaffected.

While nearly ninety percent of my total field of view is unaffected, the amount of information that is lost is far greater. To get a sense of this, focus on something like a calendar or a clock on the wall. Notice how sharp or clear the image is. Then focus on a spot twenty or thirty degrees to the right or left. Without shifting your eyes, can you tell what time it is or read the calendar? Our peripheral vision is good for detecting motion and seeing at night, but it provides nowhere near the clarity and vivid colors of our central vision.

Fortunately, today I still have a tiny island of cells at the very center of the macula in my left eye. There are virtually no good cells in my right. To get a sense of my eyesight, take that salad plate and imagine a small hole in the middle of it so you can see through to what's behind it. That is all I can see clearly. For example, when I sit across the dinner table from my wife, I can see only one of her eyes clearly. Everything else is blurry. To see her entire face, I must scan left, right, up, and down to capture it all, but I can never see her entire face clearly. Marilyn has a huge smile that lights up a room. It is one of the things I fell in love with the moment I met her. Today, the best I can do is capture bits and pieces of it, and as the few remaining cells in my left macula die, my central vision will continue to narrow until all that is left is my peripheral vision and only the memory of her beautiful smile.

To get a better idea of the effects of macular degeneration, search "macular degeneration what do you see" on Google Images.

It isn't completely clear how this all works. I have noticed that there are times when my brain misses things altogether. It seems to make assumptions about how to piece together the small bits of visual images it collects in my central vision. For example, the AREDS-2 supplement I take to slow the progression of my retinal disease is a large red pill. I will sometimes take the pill out of the bottle and set it on the bathroom countertop in my bathroom while I am brushing my teeth. My countertop is white. I will put the pill down knowing exactly where I put it. When I go to look for it after I finish brushing my teeth, the countertop is clear. No sign of my large red pill. Just white surface. How is that possible? I put it right there. But I have learned to keep scanning because I know it's there. I just haven't been able to align any of the remaining cells in my macula with the red pill. As I scan the countertop it will suddenly appear, right where I'd left it. Right where I had looked in the first place.

Apparently, when my brain looked at the countertop it saw a large white surface. The pill was in one of the dead spots. My brain must have made an inaccurate guess that there was nothing else there of interest and didn't scan as thoroughly. I have also noticed that when there is a lot of movement my field of vision seems to narrow even more. My brain seems to be collecting as much information about the movement as it can and there is less information collected elsewhere. It's why I no longer drive. It would be too easy to miss a slow-moving pedestrian crossing the road.

I was scared when I was first diagnosed with macular degeneration, but it didn't become real to me until I started to experience the effects of losing my central vision. At first the changes were minimal. Today my vision has been seriously compromised. With each dying cell, I have learned just a little more about myself. In that way, it has been somewhat of a blessing. Not one I would have wished for, but certainly one I have benefited from. I can look back now at many of the most difficult times in my life and see clearly the role that my lack of emotional awareness has taken on me. Some of those challenges have been far more consequential than others, but even in the smaller ones I see opportunities to grow.

One of the best examples of a small challenge that had major learning opportunities for me came on a business trip I took a couple of years ago from Denver to the East Coast. I was meeting with a few executives with an insurance company we had done business with for the last ten years. They had decided to put the business up for a competitive bid and we went out to present our case on why they should stay with us.

As I boarded the plane, all the window shades were drawn to keep the plane cool, so the plane was dimly lit, which makes

Seeing Clearly

it difficult for me to see anything in detail. I knew that the row numbers on United aircraft tend to jump around a bit and it was never exactly clear, to me at least, what the numbering scheme was on any model. This one was a Boeing 757-200. Rows one through four were Business Class. Economy Plus started at row seven, but only on the left side of the plane—it started at row eight on the right. There was no row five or six anywhere and no row seven on the right side. From there the rows continued back through row twelve and then suddenly, for no clear reason except to skip the unlucky row thirteen, they jumped to row twenty. Economy Plus ended at row twenty-two, where the Economy section continued all the way back to the last row, number forty.

Even with perfect vision it takes careful attention to detail to understand. I am sure this makes great sense to some bureaucrat at United but, clearly, he or she is not visually impaired or doesn't fly.

At the time, I traveled a lot for business, so I was usually able to confirm a reservation toward the front of the plane in the Economy Plus section. At six-foot-four I cherished the extra legroom. On this flight I was in 9D, an aisle seat on the right side of the plane, somewhere near the front.

As I boarded the plane, I started looking for the placement of the row numbers. It was clear that in the dim lighting it was going to be hard to see them, but if I could find one, I could then follow the line to the next printed number and the next and the one after that until I found my row. With United's ridiculous row numbering scheme, it would do me no good to just count the number of rows I passed on the way back to my seat.

I knew my seat was near the front, so I did not have a lot of time to get oriented before passing my row. If I could just keep my eyes focused on where the row numbers were printed as I moved down the aisle, I would have no problem finding my seat. Try as I might, I could not find a row number anywhere. I just couldn't line up the printed row numbers with any of the remaining cells in my macula. The numbers kept falling into the black holes left by dying photocells.

I kept scanning, hoping to find at least one row number, but, to the best of my knowledge, the plane's rows were not numbered. More than one hundred thousand miles a year and you would think I would at least know where the row numbers are printed, but I just could not find them anywhere. I knew that my seat was an aisle seat on the right, but I could not remember how far back. Was it the first row of Economy Plus? I don't usually choose that because it's a bulkhead, which tends to have less storage under the seat in front. Maybe it was the second or the third row in Economy Plus. *Why the hell didn't I check the seat map before I got on the plane?*

As I walked slowly down the aisle, I kept searching for row numbers. No luck. Not a single number. I knew it couldn't be too far back, and the last thing I wanted to do was pass my seat and then have to walk back against the flow of boarding passengers. In my head, I could already hear the other passengers saying, "Pay attention, dude. What are you, stupid or blind?"

As I approached the second row of seats in the Economy Plus section, I realized I had no choice. I had to ask someone for help. Over a million and a half miles flown in my lifetime and I couldn't find my seat by myself. *Am I really that helpless?* I couldn't help but think how crazy it was that I was flying halfway across the country to try and convince someone they could trust me with more than ten million dollars a year in business when I couldn't even find where I was supposed to sit on the flight out.

I turned to the gentleman behind me. "Do you see a row number? I am not sure where row nine is."

"It's right here, man," he said, with a very curious tone, pointing to the number directly in front of my face.

Seeing Clearly

"Thank you." I sat down feeling frustrated, helpless, and embarrassed.

The next evening, on my return flight, I was in the same seat and found it without incident. I had not had time to eat before boarding the plane, so, after take-off, I picked up the in-flight magazine to see what options I had for a meal. Since it was a night flight the lighting was low in case passengers wanted to sleep. Even with my overhead light on it was impossible for me to read what the options were, so I put the magazine back and waited for the flight attendant.

"Thank you, Mr. Monnette, for being a 1K member. Can we get you a complimentary snack?" the flight attendant asked when he got to my row.

"Yes, thank you. What do you have?" I asked. I didn't want to say I tried but couldn't read the list of options. That would be just too embarrassing. My ego was bruised enough already just from trying to find my seat the day prior.

The flight attendant reached down and pulled the exact same magazine I had already attempted to read from the seat back pocket in front of me. He flipped it open to the list of meal options and handed it to me without saying a word. I looked at the page for a few minutes as if I were studying my choices, but what I was really doing was figuring out if I was going to say "I changed my mind; I'm not hungry" or "I will have the cheese plate." They always have a cheese plate.

As I sat there looking at the magazine deciding which way to go, the woman seated in the middle seat next to me pointed to something on the page and said, "I had that the other day, and it was pretty good. The humus is great. I have had the hamburger and it is horrible and the tacos are soggy. This one isn't bad."

"Thank you. That looks great," I said to her, although I had no idea what she was actually pointing to. It was little more than a blur to me.

The flight attendant, who was standing there observing the entire interaction, realized that I had decided, and asked simply, "Which one?"

"I'll have the humus," I said, repeating the one word I remembered her saying.

"Can you give me a humus snack box?" he asked the flight attendant on the other side of his cart.

When my seatmate heard the exchange between the two flight attendants she spoke up and said, "No, he doesn't want the humus snack box. He wants the other thing, the meal."

"Oh, that! Yeah, that's pretty good." He grabbed the correct meal and set it down on my tray table without saying a word and moved on to the next row.

"Thank you," I told the lady next to me. I wanted to explain the situation to her, but I was too embarrassed, and I knew she would rather just enjoy her movie than hear my sad-luck story.

"You are welcome. I fly nearly every day, so I have tried them all. I hope you enjoy it." She put on her headphones and went back to her movie.

I looked down at the meal in front of me and suddenly there was a new problem. I had no idea how to open the plastic container it was in. I started pulling at different parts of the plastic hoping that it would miraculously open. The whole time I was thinking, *Dear God, don't dump this in her lap.* I eventually got the package open and began to scan the contents of my meal. There were three little compartments. On the right was what appeared to be some type of rice mixture. The one on the lower left looked like it might be mashed potatoes; I assumed that was the humus. The upper left was something dark brown and solid. I had no idea what that was. For a moment I thought about asking my seatmate, but she was engrossed in her movie and how could I ask her what was in front of me after I'd "read" the description she had pointed to in the magazine?

I decided I would start with what I knew. I stuck my fork into the rice and took a bite. She was right—it was pretty good. I really didn't like humus, but I figured if the rice was that good, maybe the humus would be okay. I decided to give it a try next. I stuck my fork into the lower left compartment and felt something firm. I poked at it a couple more times with my fork until I was able to pick it up. That's when I realized that I had speared a piece of pita bread, not humus. I pulled it off the fork with my fingers and ate it. Bread and some form of wild rice. That left just the contents of the top left to explore. It looked like a brownie, and it made sense there would be a dessert, but where was the humus?

I guessed it was mixed in with the rice. I had a little more rice and then another piece of pita bread before I decided to give the brownie a try. I poked at it with my fork. It was hard but broke without too much difficulty. The inside seemed a bit too soft for a brownie. As I poked at it more, it seemed like a giant hushpuppy. With the help of my fingers and the fork I was able to get a small piece into my mouth. It wasn't a brownie or a hushpuppy. I had no idea what it was, but it wasn't bad, so I ate it. I finished my meal and somehow managed to pack everything back up without dropping it in my lap or on the woman next to me. I handed it to the flight attendant as he passed through the aisle to pick up the trash.

The next morning, I was at home, sitting in our kitchen recounting the story to Marilyn, and she picked up her iPhone to do a quick Google search of in-flight meals on United flights to see if we could figure out what I'd had. As she looked at the results of her search, she said, "You apparently had a Mezze Sampler."

"What's that?" I asked.

"It is a Greek-style ancient grain salad with roasted tomatoes, cucumber, kale, peppers and red onion, it was served with falafel and flatbread."

"Falafel. Of course! I knew it wasn't a hushpuppy. I guess I like humus after all."

That trip would have been a lot easier for me if I had been willing to be vulnerable and ask for help, but that has never been how I was wired. That was more than two years ago and today my eyesight is far worse. With each passing day it has gotten harder for me to handle many of the routine things that I have taken for granted, and I have been all but forced to start taking chances with being vulnerable with others.

Several months ago, I went to see my doctor for a routine physical examination. When I checked in, the woman behind the counter gave me an iPad with instructions to fill in my medical history and insurance information. I sat in a chair fumbling with the iPad for several minutes. I couldn't read anything, and the interface was far from intuitive, at least for a guy with poor eyesight. I was getting madder by the moment. *I've been coming here for years. They already have this information. Why the hell do I waste my time on this stupid shit?*

Then I heard Marilyn's voice in my mind. "Just ask for help. You will be surprised at how many people actually want to help." God knows how many times she has told me that. I sat there for a moment knowing that at some point I would have to tell them I couldn't complete the simple task requested so there was no use sitting there being mad at the world. I walked up to the lady and said, "Excuse me. Can you help me with this? I am visually impaired and cannot read it." It was the first time I had ever used the term "visually impaired" with anyone other than my family or closest friends. I imagine I sounded so timid. As silly as it sounds, it was one of the hardest things I have done in a while. She looked up at me for a moment—I could tell she was confused—then smiled and

Seeing Clearly

said, "Of course." She walked over and sat in a chair next to me and together we completed the required forms. She was so sweet and helpful. Marilyn was right, all I had to do was ask for help.

What is more than a little silly is that I have been unwilling to be open about my disability out of a fear of being judged poorly, yet how many times have I fumbled around trying to hide it, like on those flights? The question I eventually had to ask myself was: Would I rather be judged for not being able to find my seat on a plane or for having a disability that is beyond my control? It seems like that should be a simple choice. I need to learn to trust people more. In a very real way, it is only through being more vulnerable with others, and asking for help when I need it, that I will be able to achieve the very things that will make my life easier.

I took a big step in this direction. It was getting harder and harder for me to work with my computer, and my visual challenges were starting to get in my way with keeping up with the demands of my job. This was a far bigger issue than just asking for help from the receptionist at my doctor's office. This had a direct impact on my livelihood, and I was nervous about saying anything, but it had reached a point where I had to do something or I would be unable to keep up. I finally went to my boss and explained the situation. I told him that I still felt more than capable of doing my job, but I needed some assistance in terms of technology to help me with working on my computer. It was a big step for a guy like me. I had to be vulnerable and admit I needed help. I could not have asked for a better reaction. "Chris, I really appreciate you coming to me with this. You contribute so much here. We don't want to lose you. How can I help you?" The company ended up investing in a new computer, a larger monitor, and specialized software to help me be more productive. It was a huge help for which I will be forever grateful.

The good news is that I am learning to be more vulnerable and trusting of others, and to ask for help when I need it. It hasn't come easy for me, and I doubt seriously that I would have ever learned that on my own. It took a chronic disease to rob me of much of my eyesight for that to happen.

My journey is just beginning—there is so much more for me to learn—but with each step in that direction, my life gets easier. The loss of my parents was unquestionably a devastating blow to me, particularly considering that I was already struggling with an impending career failure. While incredibly painful, their deaths were unavoidable. On the other hand, the devastation to my family in the years that followed her passing was completely avoidable, which made it that much more painful for me. The answer wasn't a hard one. All I had to do was ask for help, but that was a lesson I had yet to learn, and there are few more memorable lessons in life than the ones learned through pain.

12

Rock Bottom

One day, not long after Mom died, I came home from work and found my father sitting in his study, lost in thought with a blank expression on his face. He had Mom's urn in his lap, and he had taken the top off and was letting her cremated remains sift through his fingers. I walked in and sat in the recliner next to him.

"Dad?"

He glanced up at me briefly and said, "Can you believe this is all there is?"

"No, I can't, Dad." I had no idea what else to say.

He closed the urn and sat it down on the table between us and we sat there in silence for a minute or two, each lost in thought.

"I went to Olive Garden for lunch," he said.

"That sounds nice. I know you like that."

He seemed so distant. Another minute or so passed before he said softly, "I don't know if I can do this."

"Do what, Dad?"

"I barely made it to the end of the street before I had to pull over to the side of the road. I just sat there and cried. I couldn't drive."

I couldn't believe the words I had just heard. I had never known my father to be so emotional, and it was painful to hear.

"Oh, Dad, I am so sorry. It's hard, I know, but you will get through this."

I will never forget his next ten words.

"What's the use, Chris? I don't want to live anymore."

For a moment I couldn't breathe. I searched for words. "Dad, you have to," I pleaded.

He looked up at me and asked softly, "Why?"

It was like watching a giant oak wither and die right before my eyes. For all my life I had seen my father as a symbol of unimaginable strength, something I could only aspire to, and at that moment he seemed so frail and weak. I had no idea how to respond; I just wanted him back the way I had known him for all my life. I hated to see him in such pain, and I hated how it made me feel. It was far easier for me to ignore the sorrow I felt in my own heart when he was stoic and unemotional. In all the years I had known him, that was the most vulnerable and honest expression of his emotions that I had ever experienced, and I just wanted it to end. I desperately searched for an answer and all I could find was, "You have to, Dad. For me. For Mike. For your grandkids." I no longer remember the conversation that followed, but what I do know is that I did everything I could to get the conversation back to safer ground. At the time I am sure I would have said that I was trying to move on to help ease his pain, but the reality is that I hated the emotional territory we were in, and I just wanted to run as far away from it as I could.

The days following Mom's death were a turning point in my relationship with my father. We became closer than any other time in my life, which today I attribute largely to seeing his vulnerability. It helped me understand him better. I think that as a child I felt emotionally neglected by my father, which for years I attributed to

Seeing Clearly

the fact that he just didn't love me that much. I can see how, as I got to understand him more, I began to realize that whatever emotional neglect I felt was due only to his inability to express his emotions, not a lack of love for me.

That understanding of my father also provides insight into my relationship with Holly. She is much like my father in terms of the ability to access and express her emotions, and I can see how I would find that type of a relationship safer, given my own discomfort with emotions. As a result, however, it seems almost inevitable that we would both feel unfulfilled in our relationship. Like the relationship with my father, that lack of fulfillment wasn't the result of absence of love, rather the absence of emotional intimacy.

Not long after my mother died Holly and I finally reached a point with our entrepreneurial venture, Caffé Botanica, where we either had to take what little money we had left in our savings and use it to keep the company alive or admit that we had failed and walk away from all that we had invested in the business. That's when we had the first bit of good luck in more than two years. A large multinational company announced that they would be opening a location on the other side of town, and I was offered a job leading the startup of the operations there. It was a great job offer that came along exactly when we needed it. We pulled the plug on Caffé Botanica, and I accepted the job in July 2005. Our life seemed to be back on track again, but as it would turn out nothing could be further from the truth.

In late August of that year my new boss asked me to fly down to Miami for a meeting. As I was going through security at the airport in Oregon I ran into a relatively new colleague of mine, Carol. We had worked together previously, and I had recommended her for the job shortly after I joined in July. By coincidence, she too was on her way to Florida to meet with her new boss. Also headed to South Florida that week was Hurricane Katrina.

By the time we got to the hotel in Miami that night it was clear that the storm was not going to miss south Florida and our company closed their corporate offices in Miami. All outbound flights were booked solid, so our only option was to wait out the storm at the hotel where we were both staying.

There was a small restaurant in the lobby and not much else. The next day, as the brunt of the storm passed through, Carol and I met for lunch in the hotel. I can remember looking out the window and seeing the rain blowing sideways. There was no way we were going anywhere and no one with our company was working, so we decided to have a drink and catch up. We sat there for hours and downed several glasses of wine when suddenly I saw a flirtatious smile come across her face and she said, "Something tells me we're going to be fucking like rabbits later."

I was shocked! I vividly remember the thoughts that went through my mind at the time. *I cannot believe you just said that. Why would I want to have sex with you? I'm happily married.* I almost laughed at first because I assumed she had to be joking, but the look on her face said otherwise. I was literally speechless. And embarrassed. I was trying to think how to say "I am not interested" without offending her. I think the response I came up with was simply, "Okay," and we headed upstairs with almost no further conversation. I remember walking toward the elevator thinking, *What the hell am I doing?* When we got in the elevator, she kissed me. I think that if we were still in the lobby when that happened it might have been enough for me to come to my senses and walk away, but the elevator door opened and her room was right there. We spent two nights together before flying back to Oregon after the storm passed.

I have been judged harshly by many, including myself, for my actions and I have never denied that what happened was wrong. What frustrated me for years is that I could never explain why it happened in the first place. My marriage was not perfect, but if asked I would have, without question, said that I was in love with my wife. There was also no doubt that I was far more physically attracted to Holly than I ever was to Carol, yet I still got in that elevator with Carol that day. It has only been recently that I have discovered some sense of why.

There was a huge hole in my heart from the loss of my mother as well as the successive failures in my career. That had left my feelings of self-worth at an all-time low. I do not know if I was unaware of the emotional burden I was carrying at the time or if I was simply ignoring it. Either way, it left me feeling unfulfilled in my life, and then suddenly there was someone who wanted me. On some level, I imagine, I thought, *This will fill that hole inside me.* It didn't. In fact, it only made it deeper, but it would take time and a lot of pain for me to realize that.

I would love to say that my relationship with Carol ended when we left Florida. It didn't. It continued for two months before my guilt became too much for me to live with. I knew that I could not go on with the way things were. Something had to change. Looking back on those days, I can see how I began to see nothing but fault with my wife, whereas Carol could do no wrong. It is amazing, when you look hard enough for something, good or bad, you can usually find it, whether it is there or not. Subconsciously, I began to build a list of all the reasons why my relationship with Holly was flawed. Today, I cannot come up with a single reason why I thought Carol would be a better partner to go through life with than my wife, other than our similar interest in music.

In November 2005, Carol and I decided we would leave our

spouses and pursue a relationship together. Carol divorced her husband in less than a week. There was no separation. Just a speedy divorce. Apparently, the State of Oregon allows a same-day divorce if it is uncontested and there are no minor children involved.

I told Holly I wanted a divorce at about the same time Carol told her husband. For us, a speedy divorce was not an option. Our children were eight and eleven. I no longer recall the reasons I gave Holly—or anyone else, for that matter. I think it may have been simply that I was unhappy, which was true, although I cannot say I was unhappy with Holly or that it was her fault. I just knew I wasn't happy.

I found a small apartment not far from where we lived and moved in a week or two later. I did not live there long. The affair with Carol ended in January as abruptly as it started and with even less conversation. It was suddenly just over, without so much as a goodbye. I cannot even say, with any degree of certainty, who ended it. All I know is that I was suddenly back with Holly and Carol remarried her husband, almost as fast as she divorced him.

Fortunately for me, Holly was willing to give me a second chance and we started the long journey of rebuilding trust between us. We attended Imago Relationship Therapy, which was primarily focused on conflict resolution skills. It did not feel right to me at the time, and looking back now it seems clear that that course of therapy was a mistake. Not that we could not benefit from better conflict resolution, but I left there with no clearer picture of why I chose to cheat on her in the first place, nor did Holly and I learn to be any more vulnerable with each other in the process. Three years later, that would prove to be catastrophic.

Holly and the kids were not the only ones who were hurt by my affair with Carol. My father was squarely in the middle of it as well. When I moved out in November 2005 Dad was still living in the house with Holly and the kids. At first, Dad was very critical of my decision and rightfully so, but somewhere along the way he decided it was all Holly's fault. He began to criticize her for allowing our relationship to fall apart all while living under the same roof with her. I do not know what was going through his mind, except that I imagine he was trying to be supportive of me. Whatever the reason, it was not long before I got a rather heated call from Holly.

"Chris, your father has to go! I cannot have him living in the same house with me. I want him out NOW!"

"What happened?"

"He has started blaming me for us splitting up. How the hell is that my fault? You are the one who cheated on me! What did you tell him?"

"What? I don't understand. I told him the truth," I said.

"Well, whatever it is I want him out and I want him out now. He can come live in your apartment."

"You know I don't have room here. That just can't work."

"I don't care. That's not my problem. Get him out."

"Okay. Let me call Mike and see if he can move to Texas with him."

A week or two later, Dad was on his way to Dallas.

My relationship with my father had grown more in the ten months following the death of my mother than it had in the previous forty-six years. Having him basically chased out of the only home he had infuriated me. I wanted to blame Holly, but in my heart I knew I was to blame. It was simply another casualty of my actions.

I would only see him a couple more times before he died after falling and hitting his head on his eighty-second birthday. I flew to Texas one last time to see my father after his fall. He was in a nursing home, and it was hard not to think back to my mother's last days. It was a different facility two thousand miles away, but it was just too familiar. This time, I wasn't fooling myself like I did with Mom. I knew there would be no recovery. This was the end of the road for my father.

On the last day I spent with him, I sat by his bed alone with my thoughts and watched him lay there staring off into some unknown place. I thought back on all that we had gone through over the last two years since my mother's stroke. For all my life, I had loved him, and at times feared him. I had spent half a century trying to live up to his expectations and always feeling as if I came just a bit short. Now through the distance of time, I realize that it was my own expectations of myself that I had failed to meet. He was always far prouder of me than I ever was of myself. I tried so hard to be the man he was and lost sight of the man I was in the process.

Just before I was about to fly home to Oregon, I leaned forward and quietly said something I have no memory of ever saying to him previously: "I love you, Dad." Can that really be the only time I told him that?

He died on May 21, 2007. Holly, the kids, and I flew to Texas for Dad's memorial. It was a small and somber event with a military honor guard in recognition of his thirty years in the Navy. I was nowhere near as emotional at my father's memorial as I was for Mom's. It is hard for me to say with any degree of certainty why, except that the two years leading up to that day had been one of the most tumultuous periods of my life. I think I was more numb than anything. It may have also been the presence of the military honor guard, which somehow reminded me of the importance of keeping my composure. The only thing I can say with certainty is that the hole inside me grew even deeper that day, and yet I was still so certain I had everything under control.

Over the next year, life for Holly, the kids, and me seemed, on the surface at least, to get back to normal, but I had yet to spend any time looking inside to understand what had led me to the affair in the first place. I was more than willing to just chalk it up to a

Seeing Clearly

stupid mistake. The one thing I knew for certain was that I would never do anything so stupid again. No, I would be even dumber this time around.

I first met Rachel in September 2005 when I hired her, only a few weeks after Carol and I returned from Miami. For the first three years that I knew Rachel our relationship was friendly and strictly professional. I enjoyed her humor and her drive. We worked together well and became friends. Then in late August 2008, almost exactly three years after the storm in Miami, everything changed. At first it was a few seemingly innocent flirtatious comments by her, but in the space of a single day they quickly became explicit, and then physical. I remember the day well. It was my sixteenth wedding anniversary, which underscores just how lost I was at the time.

By late October 2008, just as with my first affair, my guilt about my relationship with Rachel was beginning to overcome me. I felt trapped in the situation I had allowed myself to get into. Holly had been willing to take another chance on me after my first affair, but she would rightfully never do that again. I either had to call it off with Rachel or walk away from a marriage of sixteen years. Just as it was with my first affair, I could not explain why I was so unhappy with my marriage, but the fact that I was now having a second affair seemed to be proof to me that there was some unknown fundamental flaw in our relationship. I convinced myself that Carol and Rachel were clearly signs that I needed to quit lying to myself and move on.

There was at least one other option that I never considered. I could seek professional help from a therapist and invest the time and emotional energy to find out why I felt so much discontent. The fact that I never considered that is not a huge surprise to me now. I was never one to ask for help. I do not know if that would have saved our marriage, but I would have preferred the decision of whether or not to walk away from my marriage to be a mindful one rather than one of ignorance that resulted in so much pain for everyone. In the end, Rachel and I chose to pursue a life together. We agreed to tell our respective partners and we also agreed we would not tell them about our relationship. She would say that she was leaving her boyfriend because of his drinking. I would tell Holly that I just was not happy. Both were at least partially true.

After work one night, Rachel sent me a text message saying she had told her boyfriend and suddenly everything was real. Up until then it had seemed rather abstract, but now she was clearly expecting me to have a similar conversation with Holly, just as we had discussed. I couldn't do it. I had no idea what to say and I was filled with second thoughts. By the time we climbed in bed that night Holly knew that something was wrong. "Chris, what's up? You have hardly said a word to me all night. What's going on?"

Suddenly I was at a fork in the road. I lay there for a while staring at the ceiling trying to decide which way to go. Then I said, "I am just not happy in our marriage anymore. I think I want a separation."

"Is there another woman?"

"No! No, there isn't. I don't know. It just feels as if we have drifted apart. Things just haven't been the same since Carol. We tried but it's just not working."

After another long pause she said, "Okay. If that is what you want. It isn't what I want, but I can't make you stay."

She seemed understanding. Almost supportive. It seemed to reinforce my decision. Maybe she was feeling the same way.

"I will find an apartment someplace," I said. "It might take me a week or so to do that. We can tell the kids then."

"Okay."

With that we rolled over and tried to sleep.

Seeing Clearly

The next day, as I was leaving the house, Holly said to me, "Chris, you know I adore you, don't you?"

Her comment surprised me. In all the years we had been together I could not recall ever hearing her express her love for me so clearly. More importantly, I have no memory of ever feeling that from her. I also do not have a memory of even one deep passionate kiss between us in all the years we were together. There must have been at least a few, but I do not remember them. It was not the reason we split up, but had we been more intimate in our communications it might have helped us navigate a very difficult time in our relationship.

When we first separated, Holly and I were civil. It was clear that things would be emotional, but I thought *people get divorced all the time*. We would navigate this and maybe, in the end, Holly and I could even end up being friends just like in the movies.

I was right. It would be just like a movie: *The War of the Roses*.

Before I even had the chance to move out, I came home from work and found a pair of Rachel's shoes sitting on my dresser. I had taken Rachel for a ride on my motorcycle. She had changed her shoes for the ride and left a pair in the saddle bag. I am not sure how Holly found the shoes, whether it was an accident or if she went looking for evidence. Whatever the reason, everything changed. I do not know if finding Rachel's shoes and realizing that I had lied when I said there wasn't another woman was worse than if I had told her the truth in the first place. It probably did not matter as it was only a matter of time before she would have found out anyway. Either way, this time it was clear: going back would never be an option. I had burned the bridge behind me. Now there really was only one direction to go. Rachel and I moved into our small apartment, and I found an attorney. A month or so later things went from bad to worse.

Christopher T. Monnette

On Monday, December 8, 2008, my boss and the vice president of Human Resources walked into my office unexpectedly. Their surprise visit was particularly alarming since they both lived more than three thousand miles away in Miami. There was only one reason they would have shown up unannounced on a Monday morning. They were doing an investigation involving me and it took me only an instant to figure out what they were investigating. Without so much as a hello, they sat down in front of me and explained how they had received an anonymous letter regarding an ongoing relationship between Rachel and me. As Rachel's immediate supervisor I knew that was a problem. The letter also referred to another relationship I'd had with Carol three years earlier. Carol did not work for me directly, but I knew what that would say about me as the senior leader in Oregon. I admitted to my previous relationship with Carol but denied anything besides a friendly relationship with Rachel. After a handful of questions, they left my office to continue their investigation with other employees. They returned three or four hours later to present their results.

My boss began with, "We don't know what happened, Chris, but it is our determination that there is a complete lack of leadership here. You have a choice: you can resign today, and we will pay you three months of severance, or if you don't, we will fire you effective immediately. What do you want to do?"

I agreed to resign voluntarily, picked up my personal possessions, and walked out the door. Rachel and Carol had a similar fate.

To add insult to injury, the next day a reporter from the local paper called me to ask about a statement the company had sent her. It was a simple two sentence release.

"After an internal review, three employees from our Springfield call center have agreed to depart our company. While privacy concerns limit our ability to provide greater detail, we thank all

Seeing Clearly

of our employees who work daily to uphold the highest levels of professionalism." The message was clear: these three were forced out as the result of some unthinkable behavior.

The next day, the front page of the newspaper carried a headline announcing my departure along with the company's prepared statement. The timing could not have been worse. This was the height of the recession, with unemployment where we lived at fifteen percent, and thanks to the company's press release, any prospective employer in town knew something inappropriate had gone down. That would be the last job either Rachel or I would have in the state of Oregon. Then there was my divorce, which would quickly turn ugly. Had it not been for my children I would have packed my bags and left Oregon immediately. Eugene was a small town, and it was quickly becoming even smaller.

In March 2009, Rachel was offered a job as a call center supervisor with an insurance company in Golden, Colorado. It paid a lot less than what she had been making, but it was a job, and she had no option. She accepted it and agreed to move to Colorado. I did not have a single decent lead on a job in Oregon, and since Holly had not worked in years her prospects of employment were even worse. Money was running out. It was only a matter of time before I would not be able to cover the mortgage and living expenses for my children. My choices seemed clear. I could stay in Oregon until we were absolutely broke, or I could move with Rachel to Colorado where the employment market was far less bleak, but I'd be 1,200 miles away from Jonathan and Jennifer. I chose what seemed to be the lesser of two evils and agreed to follow Rachel to Colorado.

The reality of everything hit me like a truck the night before Rachel and I left Oregon. We had the truck packed and ready to go the next morning and I drove over to say goodbye to Jonathan and Jennifer. As I drove away from their home, what had been our home for the last nine years, I was completely overwhelmed with emotions. I only made it a few miles before I pulled to the side of the road and cried uncontrollably. I desperately wanted to drive back to the house and beg Holly to give me another chance, but she had made it clear that was not an option, and I could not blame her. At the time, I would have said that was the lowest point of my life, but I would have been wrong. I had farther to go before I would find the leverage it would take to get my life back on track.

I was fortunate to find a job in Colorado within the first ninety days, although it barely covered my child and spousal support, but that job only lasted a year before I was laid off again. This time it took nine months before I found my next job and my unemployment payments only covered about a quarter of the support I owed Holly. Rachel paid all of our living expenses and almost every dollar I had went to Holly and the kids in Oregon. By the time I was gainfully employed again I was way behind in support payments and the state was threatening to throw me in jail. If I thought things were tough when our coffee business was failing, I had no idea of just how bad it would get.

From the time I met Rachel until the day our relationship ended, we were little more than friends. Other than a few months in the middle there was not much of a love affair. There were just too many things working against our plans to build a life together. There were the fifteen years difference in our ages, the whirlwind of divorce lawyers, threats from the District Attorney's office about late support payments, and the constant nagging of financial pressures. Through it all, there was never a lot of spark in our relationship. The biggest problem, however, was that I still felt the same discontent. If anything, our relationship had only made it greater. There was still that hole that I had been unable to fill and with each day it only seemed to get bigger.

Seeing Clearly

Our relationship finally ended in the summer of 2011. Rachel had once told me that she had never left a relationship without cheating. To the best of my knowledge her track record is still intact. In August, she had driven to Las Vegas with several friends to see a concert. When she returned, she told me that she had slept with another man while she was there, that she was in love with him, and was leaving me. He was her age, he wanted to have children, and I did not, and just to add a little more sting to it she pointed out that in the three years we had been together she had noticed signs of me aging and she did not find that attractive.

I guess it is true: Karma's a bitch.

That's when I finally realized I had hit bottom. I was far worse off than ever. I was almost completely broke, I was alone, and I was more than 1,200 miles away from my children. Everything that I had given up to be with Rachel flashed through my mind: my children, my marriage, my job, my home, my friends in Oregon. The list went on and on. I was fifty-two years old and with each passing year things seemed to be getting worse, not better.

Some people look for happiness in drugs, alcohol, food, or shopping. For me it was other women. My marriage may not have been perfect, but the source of my pain wasn't my wife. It was the loss of both of my parents, combined with my career and financial woes of our failing business. There is no doubt that those years were a difficult time for me and my family, but I somehow lost track of just how lucky I was until it was too late. That's when I knew for certain that I needed professional help or the next chapter in my life might be a disaster I could not survive.

13

Long and Winding Road

The day after Rachel and I broke up, I started looking for a therapist. My criteria were simple. I needed someone who had an office within reasonable driving distance, someone I could afford, and someone who could see me right away. I had a problem to solve, and I was not planning to waste any time doing so. I was in task mode. The night before I met with my new therapist, Brent, I sat down in front of my computer to outline a few topics for our discussion. I wanted to make sure that he had all the relevant information from the last several years so that our conversation would be productive right from the beginning. As I wrote, my sentences turned into paragraphs and paragraphs into pages. I worked on my notes well past midnight before I finally felt I knew what I needed to cover with him the next day. When I finished early that morning, I felt good about what I had written. It was well laid out and it was complete. This was going to be a big help in jump-starting our discussion.

Brent was warm and friendly. He had a calm, casual style that was probably just what I needed. I could tell right away that he was someone I would feel comfortable talking to.

Seeing Clearly

"How can I help you?" he asked after we had settled down in our respective chairs.

"I made a few notes," I said. I reached into my jacket pocket and pulled out what I had written the night before. As I extended my arm toward him with the neatly folded pages in hand I suddenly noticed, seemingly for the first time, the magnitude of my work. Six typewritten pages, ten-point font, single spaced.

He reached out to take the document and for just a moment we both held it and looked at each other.

"Would you like me to read it?" he asked.

"Ah, well, it's a lot, sorry. I mean, I guess. If you want to." I finally let go of the pages.

Brent sat back, crossed his legs, and began to read. It is amazing how slowly time passes while you watch somebody read. Every so often he would look up at me and nod or raise an eyebrow and then return to the tome in his hands.

After what seemed like an eternity, he neatly folded the document and handed it back to me. He leaned back in his chair, smiled, and simply said, "Wow, that was a lot."

I felt lost and completely unlovable the day I walked into Brent's office. I had no explanation for all that had happened in my life over the last several years. I certainly knew the facts, but I was completely ignorant as to why I had made such bad choices. How could I ever find lasting happiness like that? And who in their right mind would even consider a relationship with a guy with my track record?

What is ironic is that while I was blindly cheating on my wife, I was busy at work preaching the virtues of "The Five Whys," an iterative process developed by the Toyota Motor Company that involves asking "Why?" repeatedly until a root cause for a particular issue is identified. If I ever asked myself "Why?" I almost certainly never asked a follow-up question.

Why would I even consider cheating on my wife?

Because I am not happy.
Okay. Makes sense.

In the year I spent with Brent we may have made it to one or two more "Whys," but human behavior isn't like machinery. Understanding the root cause is not a linear process. It took macular degeneration and my work with my second therapist, Chad, to start to unwind the tangled ball of emotions that led me down the path I chose.

In January 2012 a good friend of mine, Cheryl, introduced me to a client of hers who lived in Boulder, Colorado. It was almost an hour's drive from where I lived and if it had been anyone else suggesting it, I would have passed, but Cheryl is more a sister than a friend. At the time, I would have said she knew me better than any woman in my life, except my mother. I made plans to meet her client, Marilyn, the following Sunday for brunch.

When Marilyn opened the door, I was immediately captivated by her warm, genuine smile. She is someone who smiles with her whole face. An authentic smile that in an instant gives you a view into her soul. I remember thinking, *Wow, I guess I am going to have to get used to the drive up to Boulder.*

"Chris, hi! Come on in, I am almost ready." She gave me a warm, welcoming hug.

"Thanks. It is so nice to meet you in person." We had spent an hour on the phone talking earlier that week.

"You too."

"Marilyn, I hope you don't mind, I made reservations at Brasserie Ten Ten for 11:45?"

"Are you kidding me? I wasn't sure if you were familiar with Boulder, so I made a reservation at Brasserie Ten Ten as well."

"Really! That's so funny. I'd thought about Pizzeria Locale, but figured a French bistro sounded more appropriate for a first date."

"Oh my God! Are you serious? That was my second choice."

The connection between us was almost instant. We have been together since that day and, God willing, we will be together for the next thirty years or more. Cheryl officiated our wedding at Chautauqua Park in Boulder eighteen months later on July 13, 2013. My vows that day began with,

"Marilyn, I remember as a young boy when my family would go on road trips it was not uncommon for Dad to take 'shortcuts' that turned out to be not so short. While it was not uncommon for us to take the road less traveled, we always seemed to get to where we were going even though there were times that all of us, except my father of course, had our doubts.

"As I stand here today that feels like such a perfect metaphor for my life. It has been a long and winding road for sure. So, maybe it was luck or perhaps fate, but as I look back now this is exactly where I was always headed."

As I reflect on my vows that day, I find it interesting how my words seemed to suggest that I saw that day as a destination, the end of a long road, rather than a waypoint on a never-ending journey, something that would be driven home just around the next bend as my view of the world around me began to blur.

My life's journey has always been about getting to a destination. Life will be great when... What I can see now as I look back over the road I have traveled for more than six decades is just how many times I moved the destination. Wherever I was on the road, all I could see was what might be around the next bend and all my energy was focused on getting there. I rarely, if ever, noticed just how often I not only reached a destination, but blew right past it without even realizing, because I was focused on the next one. If you aren't happy where you are, how can you be so sure you will be happy somewhere else? That is a question I never thought to ask myself until recently.

It wasn't that long ago, while trying a new guided meditation, that the instructor asked, "What is the one thing you most want in life, one word or phrase? The first thing that comes to your mind."

I was shocked how quickly and dramatically the word jumped into my mind: *Peace*. It was not something I remember ever thinking about before. I even went back and tried on all the usual ones—health, happiness, security, wealth—but none of them was as brilliant in my mind as peace. Given how bad my eyesight was, I found it, on the surface at least, surprising that the first word that came to mind was not "vision" or even "health."

In hindsight, it makes sense. If you cannot be content with where you are and are constantly being pulled forward to a destination you may never reach, how could you ever feel at peace?

One of the ways that Marilyn and I are very different is how we look at the future. For example, I am constantly evaluating our finances and planning for our retirement. I round up on every expense and down on income projections. My analysis tends to be detailed and unquestionably conservative, probably bordering on pessimistic. I am trying to look several "bends in the road" into the future. Marilyn is far more optimistic. She pays a lot less attention to my detailed spreadsheets. She believes in us, and she knows in her heart that whatever comes our way we will manage. "We will figure it out." It probably is not that hard to see which of us is more likely to experience greater peace at any given time.

I can say with absolute certainty that there is no one in this world that I would rather have by my side in this journey than Marilyn. From the day I was diagnosed she has maintained her steadfast belief that there would be a miracle that would prevent the loss of my eyesight. It is only today as I am approaching what my doctor recently described as the "end state" of this disease that I believe Marilyn is more accepting of that outcome. From the beginning, she has been pragmatic and insisted that we take every opportunity to experience life more fully while I still had most of my central vision. One of the best examples of that was a Christmas gift she gave me in 2016. It was one of the most thoughtful gifts I have ever received, and it literally changed the way I look at the world around me.

I have had a passing interest in photography for most of my life dating back to my high school years when I was the school photographer, but I had never really invested the time, energy, or money to try and pursue it as a hobby. Macular degeneration all but assured that photography was not in my future. Marilyn did not share my fatalistic view and got me an amazing camera. It turned out to be a gift that would provide so much more than a hobby.

The operation of the camera worked well with my linear mind. I loved learning all the technical issues associated with photography. I studied about the trade-offs you must make between depth of field and the amount of light you let into the camera when you adjust the aperture setting, or how shutter speed can stop motion but also reduces the amount of light the camera captures so you must be careful there is enough light in the scene you are shooting. In photography, film or sensor speed, shutter speed, aperture setting, and lens choice are interdependent. You cannot change one without thinking about at least one or two of the others. It was a math equation and I understood math.

Of course, it is not the science of photography that produces great photographs. It did not take long for me to understand why the camera is simply a tool for an artist. To capture an image that is truly captivating you first need to have something that is interesting or beautiful to shoot. Then you need to see how, or maybe better said, *feel* how to capture the image in a manner that conveys the emotion you are feeling. Understanding the science is a vital but small part of the art. I would have never described myself as an artistic person. I have always relied too much on my intellect and have rarely been able to tap into my heart, so photography turned out to be far harder than I'd ever imagined.

From the very beginning, there was a sense of urgency for me to learn all that I could about photography. The clock was ticking for me; I was keenly aware that my failing eyesight would eventually rob me of my ability to do photography. I found myself spending more and more time chasing that elusive image that would capture the emotion of being there. I was constantly scouting potential scenes to shoot. Even if we were just driving down the road and passed a beautiful setting, my mind started thinking about how to capture that image. How could I use the golden light from the rising sun to illuminate the setting? Would I be able to shoot the galactic center of the Milky Way with that mountain in the foreground at that time of the month?

I have shot thousands and thousands of images and that has resulted in a hundred that I think are special. Some of them were almost by accident. One of my favorite shots of the Milky Way was taken on a rainy night when I wanted to go back to bed, and Marilyn suggested we give it a try. That same night, I stayed up for a while after she went to bed to see what else I might get. I started walking down a dark, deserted road hoping I might find something interesting. After several minutes I gave up and decided I would head back to the hotel room and go to bed as well, but before I did, I put the camera and tripod down in the middle of the road and took one long exposure, just for the hell of it. It turned out to be one of my all-time favorite shots.

Photography has opened my mind to seeing beauty in places that I would have never looked before, such as a crowded RV park at night, a sky filled with smoke from a wildfire, or a dark and deserted dirt road on a rainy night. Along the way I have captured several images that I feel rather proud of. But that is not

Seeing Clearly

the biggest gift that I received from Marilyn's Christmas present.

I cannot help but think of the time when Marilyn and I flew out to Eastern Tennessee to spend Labor Day weekend with our friends Ron and his wife, Lynn. Ron is an amazing photographer, and he has taught me so much about the art of photography. That Saturday night, he and I hiked up to the top of Hawksbill Mountain about an hour southeast of his home in Johnson City. It is only about a mile-and-a-half hike to the top, but it climbs seven hundred feet in that short distance. It felt like a lot further carrying a backpack full of camera gear. The trip down in the dark was a bit more challenging, particularly for a guy with compromised vision. The summit is at 4,050 feet, the highest point in the Shenandoah National Park, and the views are spectacular. At the top there are large slabs of rock sticking out into space with a 2,500-foot drop to the river below.

We got to the top more than an hour before sunset to make sure we could scope out the perfect location before the sun began to set. That night I must have shot hundreds of images using every lens I had, from every possible angle, and that yielded two good images. But it is not the photographs that I cherish today. It is the experience I had with my good friend, Ron, that evening. There was nowhere else I wanted to be at that moment. There was no road in front of me with interesting bends to get to and there was no long and winding road behind me littered with painful memories. There was only that moment.

Photography has given me so many of those moments, far more than it has given me great photographs. As it turns out, Marilyn was right: A camera was exactly the right gift to give a guy who was losing his eyesight. For so much of my life I have been chasing after the next great thing, racing to get to what is around the next bend. I have rarely stopped to appreciate the view from where I was. How many wonderful experiences have I missed along the way? When I was diagnosed with macular degeneration, I was forced to accept that when it came to my ability to see the world around me clearly, what was around the next bend was worse than where I was. With that acceptance came a degree of peace.

Today when I see someone ride past me on a motorcycle, I remember my own riding experiences fondly, but I don't anguish over the loss. Even my ability to do photography has all but ended, but not my ability to admire a beautiful sunset. The one place where I have struggled the most to accept the loss has been in my career. I am just not ready to "hang up my skates," and that has caused a lot of anxiety for me.

For most of my life, my career has defined me. It has been, in many ways, a significant part of my self-worth as a man. I was taught at an early age the importance of a man's role as the provider for his family. It is easy for me to look back on my life and see that things began to change for the worse for me after I was laid off. The years following were filled with loss: the death of my parents, the loss of so much of our financial resources with the failure of our startup company, and the end of my marriage after sixteen years along with the separation from my children. The painful memories of those years are still so visceral, and I have vowed to myself I will never let that happen to me again. While I have learned to accept so much from my disability, the one thing I struggled with was how my visual challenges might adversely impact my career.

Our financial advisor is optimistic about our future, but I know that a few more years of saving as much as possible will provide even more security. In my mind the clock is ticking, and at some point I will no longer be able to perform at a high level at work and I will be forced to walk away from a great-paying job.

Since I first approached my company about my visual impairment, I have been exposed to several very helpful assistive technologies that have reduced my dependence on my visual acuity and even promise, with training and experience, to eliminate the need

Seeing Clearly

to have a computer monitor in the first place. I have met so many people who have far more significant visual impairments than me who continue to be extremely effective in corporate America today. They have been a source of both inspiration and encouragement to me. Thanks to them and the support of my company, I was beginning to feel optimistic about my ability to extend my career to a point where I would feel comfortable and ready to finally retire. But the thing about a winding road is you cannot see clearly what is really around the bend.

That is when the company I worked for announced that it was being acquired by a competitor. It didn't take a lot of research for me to see that there was more than a little chance that my position would be "redundant" in the new combined organization. In other words, there was a good chance that, when the deal closed, I could find myself unemployed at the age of sixty-three with a significant visual impairment. The prospect frightened me. I reached out to my therapist, Chad, to discuss it.

"I don't know what I am going to do, Chad. I am afraid I won't have a job in the new company, and I have no idea what I will do or want to do if I lose this job."

"Tell me something, Chris. What would be the great thing about keeping your job?"

"Well, clearly there are financial benefits."

"But didn't you tell me your financial advisor said that you would be okay?" he asked.

"Well yeah, I guess, but we would be better off two years from now and besides, you know me. I need a challenge. I am not ready to sit on the couch for the rest of my life."

"Yes, I do know you, Chris, and the one thing I am certain of is that you will find something to challenge you. That is just how you are wired. So, tell me this. What would be great about leaving this company?"

"Well, I guess it would give me the opportunity to find something that feeds my soul because this job certainly does not. It would also give me the time to finish my memoir. Maybe I would look for an opportunity to help others who are blind or visually impaired. I think we probably would be okay financially. Frankly, I would work for a fraction of my salary if I thought I was making a difference to more than a handful of millionaire executives or faceless stockholders, but I just don't think the time is right."

"Okay, Chris. I get it. The only thing I will tell you is this: Whichever path you choose to pursue, give it one hundred percent. If you want to keep this job then fight for it as hard as you can, and if you get it, then give it your all. If you choose to do something different in your life, then give that everything you have. Don't do it half-assed. Can you do that?"

"I honestly don't know if I have it in me to do that again with these guys. I worked my ass off over the last ten years and all I have to show for that is a paycheck every two weeks. There is nothing about this job that feeds my soul."

"Well, it sounds to me like you know what you want to do. I could hear it in your voice as you talked about leaving."

"I don't know, Chad. I...I just don't know. I can't just walk away."

"Why not?"

"Because, Chad..." As my voice trailed off, I found myself choking back tears.

"Can you tell me more about what you are feeling right now? Take a moment and just allow yourself to feel whatever is there."

We sat there in silence for a minute before my mind was filled with the painful memories from the years following the loss of my job, the loss of my parents, and all that followed. "I have been down this road before. I know there was a lot more happening besides being unemployed, but after I got laid off my life went to shit. The years leading up to finding this job were unquestionably

Seeing Clearly

the lowest part of my life. I vowed I would never let that happen to me again." And there it was, the real reason I couldn't just walk away. The thought of being unemployed brought back so many painful memories and feelings of loss.

As we talked through what I was feeling I felt a growing resolve inside me. I had a client who, when things went wrong, used to say, "Never waste a good crisis to make meaningful changes." Marilyn and I had prepared for this and, while the timing was not perfect, I knew it was time to heed the words of my client and make a meaningful change in my life.

After my conversation with Chad, Marilyn and I sat down and talked about what to do. I love my wife for so many reasons, not the least of which is her faith in us. "You need to do what your heart tells you and we will make it work. We can do hard things if we have to, baby."

I could not help but reflect on a YouTube video I had seen a year or two earlier of comedian and actor Will Smith talking about his first experience with parachuting out of an airplane. He describes all the fear leading up to the jump and the "blissful" experience he felt immediately after stepping out of the airplane. The moral of his story was that some of the most wonderful things are on the other side of fear.

In the end, I decided to take the jump and find out what was really on the other side of my fear.

The next day I told my boss that I didn't want to be a part of the new company, effectively closing the door on any potential continuation of employment. "I don't know what I will do next, Keith. I just know I don't want to do this. Whatever this next chapter of my life is, it will be something that feeds my soul."

"Wow! Chris. Really? Are you sure?"

"Yes. I am sure. I am scared, and I am sure."

Pulling that emotion out of the shadows has taken away some

of its power and I am able to be more objective about my path forward. I have spent far too much of my life blind to my emotions. I can look back over my life and see a trail of bad decisions and poor outcomes as a result.

If there is any one thing this journey has taught me it is that there is an enormous amount of information wrapped up in my emotions, and there is power in information. The language of emotions is not one that comes natural to me, and I am far from fluent today, but it is a journey of discovery that I am trying hard to embrace.

I do not know what is around the next bend in life any more than I did on July 13, 2013, as Marilyn and I huddled in the corner of Chautauqua Dining Hall reciting our vows. It is impossible for me to know how things may have been different in my life if it was something other than a retinal disease that awaited us, but I do know how things turned out. I am far more at peace with where I am today than ever before. Sure, I am curious, hopeful, and at times fearful about what the future might bring. Maybe tomorrow will bring a discovery that will restore the vision that I have lost, or maybe there will be a far greater challenge for me to navigate. All I can say for sure today is that I would have never wished for macular degeneration, but it was the prospect of losing something so precious as my vision that ultimately helped me begin to see what is truly important in life, and for that, I will be forever grateful.

www.ingramcontent.com/pod-product-compliance
Lightning Source LLC
Chambersburg PA
CBHW051434290426
44109CB00016B/1550